A Smarter Heart

Unlocking the Mystery of the Human Heart

By GARY LEE MEUSER

endurancepress

A Smarter Heart: Unlocking the Mystery of the Human Heart is available at special quantity discounts for bulk purchases for sales promotions, premiums, fund-raising, and educational needs. For details, write: Endurance Press, 577 N. Cardigan Ave., Star, ID 83669

Visit Endurance Press' website for additional books/resources.
www.endurancepress.com

A Smarter Heart: Unlocking the Mystery of the Human Heart
Published by Endurance Press
577 N. Cardigan Ave.
Star, ID 83669 U.S.A.

All rights reserved. Except for brief excerpts for review purposes, no part of this book may be reproduced or used in any form without the prior written permission from the publisher.

Scripture taken from the New King James Version®. Copyright © 1982 by Thomas Nelson. Used by permission. All rights reserved.

The use of italics and bold print for emphasis in quoting Scripture is the author's own.

ISBN 978-0-9964975-0-3

© 2015 Gary Lee Meuser

Cover art by Jared Meuser
Cover design and page layout by Randy Lavorante

Printed in the United States of America
First edition 2015

PRAISE FOR 'A SMARTER HEART'

"Reading *A Smarter Heart* was an insightful journey to discovering the importance of the heart. It is practical, authentic and maintains scriptural integrity. I thoroughly enjoyed the insight and I am still learning from it."
— Ben Bryson, Senior Pastor, Court Street Christian Church, Salem, Oregon.

"It would be difficult to overstate the importance of this inspiring book! It will enlighten and encourage all who study and engraft its life-changing message!"
— Mike Riddle, Accomplished and Distinguished Businessman, Salem Oregon.

"Once you begin to read *A Smarter Heart* you will find it difficult to put down. This book will inspire people from all ages and various walks of life. It is the best biblical study on matters of the heart that I have ever read."
— Pastor Rusty Huwa, Desert Shadows Neighborhood Church, Phoenix, Arizona

"I found this book to be filled with verses from the Bible that provide insight and challenge us to look not only at our own heart but also the heart of God. It is a must read for any student, minister, or lay person who yearns for a deeper understanding of the workings of the heart."
— Russell C. Spearman M.Ed. Principle Investigator, Traumatic Brain Injury Program, Idaho State University

Gary M[signature]
Prov. 4:23

PREFACE

I did not have any aspirations to write a book, being completely content preaching and teaching from the Word of God. As I discovered a wealth of facts about the "heart" in Scripture that eclipsed the recent discoveries of science on the topic, sharing these truths verbally became even more exciting. In addition I had no expertise in writing or a desire to be recognized as an author. After several sessions of speaking on the subject of the "heart" I became seriously ill with a puncture in my lower intestine. I was not expected to survive the operation, but I did, and quickly returned to teaching, unfortunately, too quickly. This was followed by several stays in numerous hospitals and many close encounters with death. Hanging between heaven and earth continued for several weeks. It seemed to me that Satan was fully committed to derailing this ministry but I was keenly aware of a "great cloud of witnesses" both visible and invisible surrounding me as a multitude of friends and family members diligently prayed and provided comfort. My wife Carolyn is at the top of the list. She stood beside me and alongside our children to provide the faith, strength and encouragement to see us all through the battles. My mother and brothers ended up extremely involved with my health crisis, praying for me and caring for me when I was unable to do so myself.

There are many physicians, nurses and other healthcare professionals, too numerable to mention all by name, that God used to keep me alive. I would like to thank Dr. Ryan Hardy, the surgeon who initially saved my life. Dr. Eric Stackle, a long time personal friend, who stepped in when there were no answers and bravely directed my health cares. Dr. Ronald Higgenbotham and Dr. Don MacDonagh demonstrated unwavering commitment to my healing. Their input has been invaluable, and I am grateful to both of them.

As noted, our Lord Jesus Christ used many people to strengthen me when I was very weak. I am convinced, as promised in the Bible, that He also personally interceded for me before the throne of God. Satan as clearly stated in Scripture is our enemy. His goal is to steal, kill and destroy. Satan did not succeed! I received the healing necessary to continue this ministry of opening the treasure of the "heart" found in the Bible and sharing it with fellow believers. Unexpectedly, writing became a key tool for accomplishing this task. This materialized when I arrived at the conclusion that just as God had made it possible for me to speak, preach and teach, He was fully capable of enabling me to write. That being recognized, allow me to emphasize that the words that should gain the readers greatest attention are not mine but rather the numerous Scriptures used in this study. If you carefully read, meditate and heed these verses, the blessings will be abundant.

Happy reading!

CONTENTS

INTRODUCTION

11	CHAPTER 1 God's Amazing Creation
20	CHAPTER 2 The Spiritual Heart
42	CHAPTER 3 Guard Your Heart
57	CHAPTER 4 An Unreliable Heart
79	CHAPTER 5 A Trustworthy Heart
95	CHAPTER 6 Live Whole Heartedly
113	CHAPTER 7 The Heart of God
133	CHAPTER 8 The Heart and Prayer
144	CHAPTER 9 God's Temple Your Heart
160	CHAPTER 10 Keeping Your Heart
191	CHAPTER 11 A Renewed Heart
206	CHAPTER 12 Coming Full Circle

AFTERWORD

INTRODUCTION

The word "heart" carries a lot of weight in our culture and around the world. Daily in our vocabulary it is used numerable times for a variety of different reasons. We often use phrases like, the heart of the matter, listen to your heart, and follow your heart. But do we really understand what we are saying? If we are to listen to our heart, how is this done? Does this mean that the heart is capable of communicating? I thought that only our brain made communication possible. Do we really intend to follow our heart when following the dictates of our mind is far more likely? There has been a tremendous amount of scientific research completed in recent decades on the heart's ability to think and communicate. These discoveries led me to search the Scriptures in depth, in hopes of uncovering even greater truths about the heart. I was not disappointed! I found that what the Bible teaches concerning the heart of man is far more profound than the discoveries of science. Obviously God already knew what man had stumbled upon. Of course He did, He created our hearts.

I was raised in the church and began my personal relationship with God through His Son Jesus Christ at a very young age. I grew in the knowledge of Christ through the instruction of Godly parents, church leaders, Sunday school teachers, Bible school professors, and many other capable instructors and authors. As I matured I was allowed the opportunity to pastor, teach and counsel in churches, high schools, and colleges. Over the years I developed relationships with a wide range of people of all ages. Out of these encounters with my fellow believers and friends grew a number of critical questions. Why do some people love God for many years and then turn their back and walk away? Why do they walk away from their families as well? Why do others seem stagnate in their spiritual growth while others appear to flourish? Why do some experience victory over many personal struggles and challenges while others rarely enjoy similar results? Why do many love their denominational theology more than fellowship with Christians of other doctrinal beliefs? Why so many church splits? Why do some Christian friendships break down, never to be resolved? Why do Christian children and parents struggle to enjoy or like each other, let alone experience love one for another? Why does so much emotional and mental illness exist? Why do some people grow old gracefully and beautifully while others grind to a halt laden with hate and bitterness? Why can't we just be happy? Yes, that sums it up! Why can't we just experience the joy of the Lord? To find the answers, and I did find them; I turned again to the Word of God, the Holy Bible. What I found was a treasure of truth wrapped up in the "heart". ***It's all about the heart!***

As we share these treasures about the heart, let's make a deal between reader and writer. Your part in this deal will be to purpose to read this book with your heart. My part was to write it with my heart. That is really what this study is all about, the importance of allowing our hearts to take the lead in all areas of our lives. I am not discounting the mind, but rather encouraging us to learn how to give the heart its proper working relationship with the mind.

Improvement in this endeavor will occur as we work our way through each chapter. This is true because we are going to study the Word of God which clearly teaches the importance of the heart with its multitude of characteristics which function in a variety of different roles. We can completely trust the Scriptures to provide the truth we desire. II Timothy 3:16 says that "All Scripture is given by inspiration of God, and is profitable for doctrine, for reproof, for correction, for instruction in righteousness, that the man of God may be complete, thoroughly equipped for every good work". The word "inspiration" in the original Greek means, "God breathed". God is the author of all Scripture, He breathed it into existence, and He watches over it with unabated intensity. Christ declared in the Sermon on the Mount that, "…till heaven and earth pass away one jot or one tittle will by no means pass from the law till all is fulfilled". In other words even the little accent marks are important. Proverbs 30:3 reminds us that, "every Word of God is pure…" Every single word no matter how small is important in understanding the full meaning of what God is purposing to teach us. By studying the Scriptures we will become keenly aware of the power of the physical, spiritual, intellectual, and emotional dimensions of the heart. We will learn how all four of these dimensions work together and how they are not easily separated.

Thank you for joining me in this adventure. It is my prayer that this study will enlarge your heart as it has mine.

Note: The use of italics and bold print for emphasis in quoting Scripture is the author's own.

CHAPTER ONE | God's Amazing Creation

"I will praise you, for I am fearfully and wonderfully made; marvelous are your works, and that my soul knows very well."

PSALMS 139:14

Years ago I received a graduate degree in Clinical Psychology. There have been a lot of changes in this discipline over the last couple of decades that actually make the study of Psychology more interesting. Because of the advancements in scientific investigation, many additional biological facts about the brain and how it operates have surfaced. I became aware of many additional physiological facts on the brain just a couple of years ago when I received the opportunity to teach several classes of Introduction to Psychology at a local Junior College.

As a study, Psychology is currently being approached in a much more scientific manner. For centuries the brain has been given the attention of great philosophers, physicians, teachers, and scientists. In the past the investigation took place examining corpses or of patients undergoing brain surgery. But now due to tremendous advances in imaging technology we can venture into the brain without opening the skull.

The February 2014 issue of the *National Geographic* magazine describes a recent advancement in "Biological Imaging" which utilize a helmet made up of a multitude of sensors. This helmet is worn by the subject being studied and provides instant feedback on specific brain functions in different regions of the brain. This is accomplished by the antennas picking up signals produced when the scanner's magnetic field excites water molecules in the brain. Computers are then used to translate this information into three dimensional pictures. Let us be reminded that this was all made possible by God. He gave men the ability to create these methods of entering the depths of the brain. And the truths we gain from their discoveries will hopefully create more awe in our souls for God's wondrous creation.

Understanding the brain will be necessary and helpful in transitioning to the mysteries of the heart. The brain is made up of billions of cells. These cells logically are labeled brain cells, and since the brain and spinal cord make up what we call the nervous system they are more specifically titled "neurons". Neurons therefore are a specific type of cell which make up the nervous system, and have their own unique appearance and characteristics.

You have probably heard the term "bean counter", well there also appears to be people who count "neurons"! They don't all agree on the total number of neurons (cells) in the brain but the number appears to range from 70 billion to 200 billion. I won't be the least bit surprised if that number increases in the years ahead as methods of discovery become more and more advanced.

When I was growing up I was left with the impression that we have a finite number of these neurons in our brains, and as the years passed on many of these neurons passed on as well. The thought was that as we entered the closing years of our life, hopefully, there would be enough remaining cells to live a half way intelligent life before dying.

Nothing could be further from the truth!

On the scene appeared a new term called "Neurogenesis" which simply means a process of regenerating new cells (neurons). This manufacturing plant resides deep within the brain and is encouraged by sleep, exercise, and stimulating environments. This phenomenon takes place at all ages of our life span, so instead of growing duller in our passing years, quite the opposite is true. We may well become brighter and more intelligent. God has given us the tools to finish well, to finish strong! Let's look more specifically at these marvelous neurons.

Neurons are basically made up of the cell body, the axon, dendrites, and neurotransmitters. The cell body is the cells' life support center and has a multitude of branching fibers, like branches on a tree. These are the dendrites which receive messages from other cells (neurons). These electrical messages are passed down the axiom, which is essentially a tube connected to the cell body. These messages travel from two to two hundred plus miles per hour to the axiom terminals, where the signals are received by another neuron. This transfer of information takes place in the synaptic gap between the neurons and that is where the signal miraculously changes from an *electrical impulse* to a *chemical reaction*. Essentially the neurotransmitters carry chemical messages across the synapses, signaling the receiving nerve cell to fire or stop firing.

We could go into this amazing information in more detail but the object here is not to write a text book on the brain but rather lay a foundation of understanding the miracle of the human brain and its relationship to the mysterious human heart. A few more facts about the brain are needed before we can transition to the heart.

The previously mentioned *National Geographic* article reveals that the current goal of research scientists is to produce a 3D mapping of the human brain. At this point they have been successful in mapping a portion of a mouse brain the size of a grain of salt. The data used to accomplish this feat is equal to that of 25,000 high definition television movies.

There are 70 million neurons in a mouse brain and one thousand times that in a human brain. Furthermore each human neuron has ten thousand synapses. Amazingly, it only takes one neuron to store the memory of your grandmother's face; even if she changes her hair color and style—you won't be fooled! The complexity and depth in each and every neuron is as difficult to comprehend as the universe itself. It appears that the inner universe of our body is as infinite as outer space. The data to map the human brain would require 1.3 billion terabytes of storage. The storage capacity available in today's world is 2.7 billion terabytes of data, nearly half the world's capacity.

In our inner cell space travel we run into its nucleus and discover a chromosome. This chromosome is made up of a coiled chain of molecules dubbed DNA. The small segments making up our DNA are genes. Genes are the very thing that makes you so much different from your friends, family, and anyone else. Biology and Psychology has also taught us that our DNA is 99.9% identical to everyone else on the planet. Perhaps we are not as different as we believe we are. But actually we are all quite unique. It is simply amazing how much diversity God can create out of one thousands of a percent.

As a result of these brain cells communicating with each other a path is created. Dozens of different neurotransmitters travel along their own pathways in the brain. They are carrying out specific but different messages that influence our behavior and emotions. As an example, Serotonin levels can affect our mood and levels of arousal. Dopamine levels influence alertness, attentiveness, and emotions. A deficiency of Norepinephrine can lead to depression. Special "mirror neurons" have a great deal to do with our ability to empathize with people, while other neurons excite our imagination.

This information about the brain is just the tip of the iceberg, but for our purposes we are not going to dig any deeper into the explanations of the workings of the brain. From this foundation we can transition to the heart and discover even greater mysteries. Scripture instructs us on all aspects of life and what sustains that life.

> "Whatever man of the children of Israel, or of the strangers who dwell among you who hunts and catches any animal of bird that may be eaten, he shall pour out its *blood* and cover it with dust; for it is the *life* of all flesh. Its *blood* sustains its *life*. Therefore I said to the children of Israel. 'You shall not eat the *blood* of any flesh, for the *life* of all flesh is its *blood*. Whoever eats it shall be cut off.'" LEVITICUS 17:13, 14

The latter portion of this passage sums up its entire meaning by declaring; "...the life of all flesh is its blood." This is a very strong declaration. That little verb "is" should not be overlooked. As we meditate on this verse, and pay close attention to the small words like "is" and "all", we are faced with an astounding truth. The life of everybody does not just come from the blood, but is the blood. And this life sustaining blood is life for every creature that God has or will create. This helps us begin to really appreciate that organ in the midst of our chest cavity, the heart. The heart, weighing only a few pounds, pumps huge quantities of life through our body from before birth until the time of death. So let's identify some astounding facts about the human heart that hopefully inspires gratefulness in us for the marvelous work God has done in creating our flesh (body).

The heart pumps approximately two gallons of blood a minute which equals 2,000 to 3,000 gallons a day. Our vascular system, the veins carrying the blood, is 60,000 miles long. If you went on a 45 year long vacation and, to your horror, left the kitchen faucet wide open; that flow of water would equal the amount of blood your heart pumps in a lifetime, totaling 1.5 million barrels. That is enough to fill up an ocean oil tanker. Perhaps, like me, you are more familiar with trains. It would require 200 train tank cars to transport the quantity of blood that your heart will pump in your lifetime if you live to old age. The heart pumps blood to nearly every cell in the body (approximately 75 trillion), except the corneas. Only five percent of the blood supports the heart. Rounding off, 20% goes to the brain, another 20% to the kidneys, and the rest to the remaining organs.

God has filled some amazing people with great wisdom and courage, enabling them to discover incredible truths about the human heart. For example, in 1929, German surgeon Werner Forssmann (1904-1979) examined the inside of his own heart by threading a catheter into his arm vein and pushing it twenty inches into his heart, thereby inventing cardiac catheterization. This now is a very common procedure in the medical field. Earlier, in 1903, Physiologist William Einthoven (1860-1927) invented the electrocardiograph which measures electric current in the heart. Through his invention researchers were able to clearly identify that the heart essentially operates as an electric pump. We will discuss later how the heart is much more than an electric pump.

The heart constantly produces between one and five watts of electricity. The heart has its own nervous system. It does not rely on the brain to function. I guess you could say it has its own breaker box. Daily within the heart, enough energy is created to drive a truck 20 miles. In a lifetime, that would take the truck to the moon and back. Because the heart has its own electrical impulse, it can continue to beat even when separated from the body, as long as it has adequate oxygen.

A mystery of the heart that we all need to grasp is that the heart has neurons just like the nervous system. It has neurons just as the brain has neurons. Some researchers have concluded that it has over 200,000; this is more than some key cognitive (thinking and reasoning) areas of the brain! As we learned earlier these neurons communicate with each other by an electromagnetic pulse which ends in a chemical response. The heart's electromagnetic field is its most powerful channel of communication, and is 5,000 times greater in strength than the brain's magnetic field.

By placing more and more emphasis on the heart I am not discounting the power of the brain. The brain and the heart work closely together. The heart beat alone is intelligent language the brain understands. The beating pattern of the heart is transformed into neural impulses that directly affect the electrical activity of higher brain centers involved in cognitive and emotional processing. The brain communicates instructions to the organs of the body. If functioning correctly they respond correctly to the commands of the brain. Dr. Colbert, in his book, *Deadly Emotions,* points out that when the brain communicates with the heart something different takes place. The heart does not immediately respond, rather it contemplates the brains message and responds to the brain with its own conclusion that the brain then cooperates with. The heart essentially regulates the mood of the entire body. Yes, this is what science has discovered. Yes, science has concluded that the heart has intelligence. And yes, God knew all along what science has recently discovered. Of course He knows — He created us!

We have concluded that the heart is more than just an ordinary pump that circulates blood. And before that, we recognized that blood is more than just a liquid; it is life to our bodies. The heart is intelligent and the blood is life. Understanding the physical attributes and operations of the body are necessary in grasping many of the spiritual truths of our existence. The physical heart is the source of life as the spiritual heart is the source of spiritual life. This will be the emphasis throughout the remainder of this book. But before we launch out into further mysteries of the heart a few more "heart" facts are needed.

In man's physical development the heart begins beating before the brain is formed. This creates a rather perplexing question. If the brain was not there to instruct the heart to beat, then how did it start? From a spiritual perspective that is easy to answer. God started the heart beating. But from a simply human point of view, man is left to conclude that since the brain did not start the heart, the heart must have started itself. In brain maturation the inner brain is formed first; which includes the brain stem, hippocampus, amygdale, etc. This is often referred to as the emotional area of the brain. Next the outer portion of the brain is formed, also known as the cerebral cortex or the rational and thinking portion. To summarize the development of our nervous system; first the heart is formed, then the inner or emotional brain, and then the outer intellectual brain. Other cultures throughout history have included both the emotional and intellectual aspects of the human heart in their thinking. For example, the Chinese symbol that describes the human heart includes the characters of "thinking", "thought", "intent", "listen", "virtue", and "love". A large number of Scriptures will be included in our study that will hopefully make it abundantly clear that God desires that His children understand and function in the full power of the miraculous heart. In the next chapter I will share a documented story that will provide strong practical evidence for the argument that the heart is intelligent. I will also cover many Scriptures from the Bible that outline the characteristics, functions, and attributes of the human heart.

PONDER THIS IN YOUR HEART

As you contemplate the miracle that you are as one of God's created children, list some things that elicit gratefulness in your heart. Now express thanks to God in prayer.

CHAPTER TWO | The Spiritual Heart

> "For the Word of God is living and powerful, and sharper than any two-edged sword, piercing even to the division of soul and spirit, and of joints and marrow, and is a discerner of the *thoughts* and *intents* of the heart." HEBREWS 4:12

When I first learned that the heart is intelligent, functioning cognitively as does the brain, and that perhaps it even trumps the brain as the leading organ in our body; I had to know what the Bible had to say on this subject. Let me make it clear at this point that my intention is to refer to a multitude of Scriptures, thus making the truths of the heart abundantly clear. To accomplish this, the wisest thing I can do is to comment on these verses in a manner that allows them to speak for themselves. I am convinced that the powerful Word of God, taught to us by the Holy Spirit, will give us the understanding necessary to appreciate and understand fully the miracle of the human heart. Particularly in our western culture, we have been taught in school from a very early age that intelligence is purely a function of our brain. When we discuss this capability, we use the term "mind". Each six or eight week period our report cards gave our parents an idea of how well our minds were maturing. Of course, this report never gave us a clue on how well our hearts were maturing.

But as science has learned in the last couple decades, the heart also has this capacity to function intelligently.

To learn the mystery of the heart, I went to the Scriptures and found that God places a high priority on the heart. I am sure that is no surprise to anyone; it is one of the most used terms in life. I was amazed to discover that the term "heart" is used approximately one thousand times in the Bible. Nearly ten times more often than the term "mind". The word "mind" does not necessarily refer specifically to our "brain"; in most cases it means "knowledge", and "understanding", and "reasoning". In the book of Proverbs, which was written to make the young man wise, "heart" is used nearly one hundred times. That is almost equal to the number that "mind" is found in the entire Bible. Almost without exception when the word "heart" is used in the Old Testament, it is the same original Hebrew word. This is also true of its Greek counterpart in the New Testament.

At first, it may appear difficult to distinguish between the physical heart and the spiritual heart. The reason for this is because it is true. It is difficult to divide our being into segments and categories. That is exactly what Hebrews 4:12 is teaching us. In fact, there are places in the Old Testament that use the same root word "lehv" for the physical and spiritual heart. One example is found in the life of King David's son, Absalom. Joab thrust three spears into Absalom's heart while he was suspended from a tree during battle. The same Hebrew word used in this passage for a physical heart is the same term used throughout the Old Testament to describe a spiritual, emotional, or intellectual heart. We are spiritual beings first and foremost. We were made in the likeness of God, who is spirit. In John 4:24 we are instructed to worship him "in spirit and truth". God, who will make our new bodies for our heavenly home, has by that same divine genius made our temporal bodies for this earthly existence.

According to Hebrews 4:12, our spirit and soul are so closely bound together that only the power of His word can divide between the two. Our joints (body) and its life sustaining marrow likewise can only be separated by Gods' mighty word. And only God can discern between the "thoughts" and "intents" of the heart. Yes, you read it correctly. According to God, our heart thinks and these thoughts at some point mature to a point of willful action. The heart makes a decision to follow through with its' own "intentions". The heart is capable of accomplishing many things. Let's look at several Scriptures that provide an overview of the hearts' attributes. Later in our study these characteristics will be covered in more detail.

THE HUMAN HEART'S CAPACITY FOR UNDERSTANDING AND WISDOM

> "I communed with my **heart** saying... my **heart** has understood great wisdom and knowledge. And I set my **heart** to know wisdom and to know madness and folly."
> ECCLESIASTES 1:16, 17

The first question I asked myself when I began reading these Scriptures on the heart was why God did not use the term "mind". Is it not the mind that is filled with wisdom and knowledge? Solomon wrote this passage and God called him the wisest man in the world. As you will see

The Spiritual Heart

later, Solomon's great wisdom and knowledge was in his heart. The author was honest in stating that he did not always use his heart correctly. He also followed the pursuit of knowing madness and folly. A lesson to remember here, we can abuse our heart and use it in an evil manner.

> "...Do not fear, Daniel, for from the first day that you set your **heart** to understand, and to humble yourself before your God, your words were heard..." DANIEL 10:12

What can be said about Daniel and his heart? Daniel has the amazing honor of not having a single negative thing said concerning him in Scripture. He was a chosen vessel of God being mightily used to influence several kings during the captivity of the Israel nation in the land of Babylon. Daniel had a great gift of interpreting dreams, even dreams that others had not shared with him previous to his interpretation. He understood the power of the human heart and purposed diligently to "set" his heart, not his mind, to acquire understanding.

> "...He has shut...their **hearts** so that they can not understand. And no one considers in his **heart**, nor is there knowledge nor understanding."
> ISAIAH 44:18B, 19

Isaiah was one of God's greatest prophets. His name means "the Lord saves" or "the Lord is Savior". The book of Isaiah contains more prophesies about the Messiah than any other Old Testament book. Augustine noted how thoroughly the book described the plan of salvation and referred to it as the fifth Gospel. Some Bible teachers have called it "the Bible in miniature". This powerful book refers to the intelligence of the heart several times, and this passage sums it up well. If God shuts up the heart, there is no hope of gaining appropriate understanding. The heart is vital in fully "considering" any situation. In fact, a closed heart negates any possible attainment of knowledge or understanding, most specifically that of the saving knowledge of Christ.

> "The **hearts** of this people have grown dull …lest they should *understand* with their **hearts** and turn." MATTHEW 13:15

Amazingly, Jesus quotes from the book of Isaiah. It is not the minds of the people which have grown dull but rather their hearts. Christ is saying that repentance is a function of the heart. Arriving at the knowledge of a savior and an understanding of His saving power becomes known to each of us through our hearts. Later on more will be said about this when we look at the tenth chapter of Romans.

THE HEART'S CAPACITY FOR THINKING, PLANNING, AND VOLITION

> "But Daniel purposed in his **heart** that he would not defile himself…" DANIEL 1:8

Daniel made a timely decision early in his captivity in Babylon. This willful decision set the tenure of his success for his entire life. The decision was made "with" and "in" his heart. How he related to King Nebuchadnezzar and the kings that followed, was set that day when he purposed in his heart to follow God. Many resolutions have been made in the minds of men; but I am convinced by Scripture that only those made in the heart contain the substance to succeed. Soon Daniel is chosen to serve the king and finds himself interpreting Nebuchadnezzar's dream. The main purpose of the dream as expressed by Daniel was "that you (king) may know the thoughts of your heart." *Not* the thoughts of his mind but of his heart. The heart thinks, or expressed differently, has cognitive ability.

> "And Mordecai told them to answer Esther: 'Do not *think* in your **heart** that you will escape in the king's palace any more than all the other Jews.'"
> ESTHER 4:13

> "So king Ahasuaras answered and said to Queen Esther. 'Who is he, and where is he who would dare *presume* in his HEART to do such a thing.'" ESTHER 7:5

Here we find another biblical record of a chosen servant of God interacting with a world leader. Esther, a Jew, was chosen to be the king's wife. Soon after they were wed, Haman, a member of the king's court, plotted to destroy the Jews. For help during this impending tragedy, her uncle Mordecai appealed to Esther's heart to make the right decision. Soon we find Ahasuaras revealing the same wisdom, recognizing that a foolish heart is behind this scheme. The word "presume" means to form a confident or arrogant opinion with the intention of following through without permission. The conclusion is that the heart is capable of thoughtfully arriving at an opinion and then by an act of volition, bringing it to pass.

> "Then Simeon blessed them, and said to Mary His mother, 'Behold this Child is destined for the fall and rising of many in Israel, and for a sign which will be spoken against '(yes, a sword will pierce through your own soul also), that the *thoughts* of many **hearts** may be revealed.'"
> Luke 2:34, 35

The most important element in relating to Jesus is not what we think of Him in our minds, but rather what place we give Him in our hearts. This is true for everyone; past, present, or future. If we just contemplate in our minds the truth of Christ, we will have a changed mind. But if man allows his heart to receive Christ, then he will have a new life. The scribes reasoned about Christ in their hearts; but not for the purpose of accepting Him, but rather to reject Him. "And some of the scribes were sitting there and reasoning in their *hearts*, 'why does this Man speak blasphemies like this? Who can forgive sins but God alone" (Mark 2:6, 7). Jesus recognized that this wrong thinking was coming from their hearts and responded in the next verse by saying: 'Why do you reason about these things in your *hearts*.'" Clearly, the most important thinking we will ever do will be done in the heart.

> "So let each one give as he purposes in his **heart**, not grudgingly or of necessity; for God loves a cheerful giver."
> II Corinthians 28:9

> "As for you my son Solomon, know the God of your father, and serve Him with

> a *loyal* **heart** and with a willing mind; for the Lord searches all **hearts** and understands all the *intent* of the thoughts..." I Chronicles 28:9

> "For the Word of God is living and powerful,... and is a *discerner* of the *thoughts* and *intents* of the **heart**." Heb 4:12

The key words to focus on from these Scriptures are "purpose" and "intent". Both words mean pretty much the same thing. If our intent is to do something, we are purposing to bring it to pass. An intention is something that a person sets before himself as a goal or object to be obtained. These Scriptures reveal that this is also a function of the heart. This ability to "think things out" does not just take place in our minds. We learned earlier, the heart reasons to the point of initiating an action. The heart kicks our "will" into gear. The intent and purpose of our heart is what we have set our face to accomplish. God alone knows our hearts. He searches our hearts and by His Spirit desires to empower us when our heart is right with him. I assure you, that when our heart is right with God, our mind will fall in line.

> "He who keeps his command (King's), will experience nothing harmful; and a wise man's **heart** *discerns* both time and judgment."
> Ecclesiastes 8:5

What exactly is "discernment"? According to Webster's 1828 Dictionary, "it is to see or discover by intellect the difference; to make distinction; as, to 'discern' between good and evil, truth and falsehood." It is the ability to distinguish or see the difference between two or more things, and to discriminate between the two, in thought or action.

This immediately brings my thoughts to Solomon. Solomon asked of God "a wise and understanding heart". The truth of God answering this prayer was shown when two women came before him with a baby, each claiming it as her own. They asked Solomon to decide to whom the baby belonged. "Divide it and give half to each!" he commanded and immediately gave it to the mother who cried out: "No!" It was God who gave Solomon a wise heart and Solomon, with his heart, made a decision that required great discernment. Many have considered this a great mental accomplishment, but truly it was a very mature act of his heart. This degree of wisdom is available to all of us who seek God for this level of heart maturity.

> "A *heart* that *devises* wicked plans..."
> PROVERBS 6:18

> "Deliver me O Lord, from evil men; preserve me from violent men, who *plan* evil things in their **hearts**..." PSALMS 140:1, 2

When discussing the stages of mental growth, the psychologist, Piaget, taught that "children are active learners, constantly trying to construct more advanced understandings of the world." Part of this active thinking is building "schemas" which are concepts or mental molds into which experiences are formed. In other words, it is a concept or framework that interprets information. Simply put, at a certain point children learn to scheme, to come up with a plan that accomplishes an end either in thought or action. To function at that level seems to be asking a lot of the heart. But it is clear in Scripture that this is exactly the case. I wonder when psychology will come to this conclusion, that schemas are also a function of a maturing heart. More Scriptures that handle this truth will be shared later. We can expect good plans (schemes) to proceed out of a good heart.

THE HEART AND MEMORY

> "Receive, please, instruction from his mouth, and *lay up* His words in your **heart**."
> JOB 22:22

> "He also taught me and said to me; "let your **heart** retain my words; keep my commandments and live." PROVERBS 4:4

> "This is the end of the account. As for me, Daniel, 'my thoughts greatly troubled me; and and my countenance changed; but I *kept* the matter in my **heart.**'" DANIEL 7:28

> "And thus, the *secrets* of his **heart** are revealed; and so, falling down on his face, he will worship God and report that God is truly among us." I CORINTHIANS 14:25

All these Scriptures reveal that the heart is a vessel of memory. We actually store memories in our hearts. I would have never considered this to be remotely possible, if the Scriptures were not so clear. There are many more Scriptures on the subject that can be added to this list. Job speaks of laying up God's words in our heart. Solomon speaks of retaining words. Daniel records his intent to keep a personal vision from God stored in his heart for later reference. The apostle Paul discusses the secrets of unbelievers' hearts being revealed as they witness the power of God during a church gathering. Before it can become a secret, it has to be stored up, and usually for quite some time.

> "My son give attention to my words; incline your ear to my sayings. Do not let them depart from your eyes; *keep* them in the midst of your **heart**." PROVERBS 4:20, 21

God has given us several ways to receive sensory information into our brains. We receive sound stimulus through our ears, and light stimulus through our eyes. Both these faculties allow us to see and hear things around us. According to this Scripture we are admonished to pay special attention to God's word. This Scripture encapsulates the steps of memory taught in science classes. The first step, "give attention" is recognizing the sound or stimulus, "incline your ear" would represent the second step of short-term or working memory, and "keep them" is the final step, or long-term memory. According to this proverb, when the Word of God is received into long-term memory it is in the "midst" of our heart. Yes, we remember things: events, conversations, memory, etc in our hearts.

And now the story I promised, that will solidify from an actual current life experience, the amazing truth of memory contained in the heart. I first became acquainted with this account in the book I mentioned earlier by Dr. Don Colbert entitled *Deadly Emotions*. A physician told this story at a conference for psychologists, psychiatrists, and social workers. She shared about an eight year old patient of hers who had received a heart transplant from a ten year old girl. In the subsequent weeks after the operation, the eight year old had ongoing nightmares of the horrible murder of the ten year old donor. She screamed in terror as she became aware of the murderer and his actions. Finally the authorities were notified and the murderer was convicted. The eight year old child knew the time, the weapon, the place, the clothes he wore, and what the little girl had said to him during the act. This was all contained in the memory of the donor's heart.

> "And all those who heard it marveled at those things which were told them by the shepherds. But Mary kept all these things and *pondered* them in her HEART." ...Then He (Jesus) went down with them and came to Nazareth, and was subject to them, but His mother *kept* all these things in her **heart.**" LUKE 2:18-19, 51

When the shepherds came to Mary, the mother of Jesus they declared to her their marvelous experience. An angel came out of heaven and had spoken with them about a child wrapped in swaddling clothes, lying in a manger. This child would be the Savior of the world, Christ the Lord. Soon a host of angels gathered around them glorifying God. Those in the stable who heard the news about Jesus "marveled", but Mary "pondered" them in her heart. There is a notable difference between these two responses, and

A Smarter Heart

Mary's response sets her apart. She rehearsed in her mind what the messengers from heaven had shared. She deliberated on the information, considering the different possible ramifications to her and her family. We would naturally conclude that this type of examination would be a mental process of our brain, but the Scripture is explicit that she "kept" and "pondered" them in her heart. Pondering information results in it being memorized. In this case it was memorized or "kept" in the heart.

Years later when Jesus was twelve years old, Mary, Joseph and Jesus took their yearly trip to Jerusalem for the Feast of the Passover. When the celebration was concluded, they began their trip with friends and relatives back to Nazareth. They were surprised to discover that Jesus was not with them. They hurriedly returned to Jerusalem to find their child. To their amazement, Jesus was in the temple asking very astute questions of the teachers, and answering their responses with great maturity. Jesus responded to his parent's concern of his insensitive tardiness by saying, "Why did you seek Me? Did you not know that I must be about My Father's business?" But instead of just being confused by Jesus' response, Mary "kept all these things in her heart."

We would do well to follow the example of Jesus' mother. To grow significantly in our understanding of Christ and His gospel, we need to be more than just amazed. Amazement is rendered to make-believe super heroes. Christ is far more than a super- hero. Christ is the almighty God, and that in itself should elicit a great deal of "pondering". He desires a personal relationship with you that continues to grow and flourish. When God does a mighty thing in your life, perhaps totally unbelievable, don't sweep it under the rug. It would be appropriate to "keep" it in your heart, not just store it in your mind. If you allow Christ to change your heart, you find yourself being used of God to change the hearts of others.

THE HEART SPEAKS

> "Now Hannah *spoke* in her HEART; only her lips moved, but her voice was not heard. Therefore Eli thought she was drunk." I SAMUEL 1:13

The truth revealed in Scripture, that the heart speaks, is explicit in understanding its power. Let's take a look at Hannah. Hannah desperately wanted a child. This communication of her heart was so profound that it appeared as though she was out of control, more specifically, as if she were drunk. This account reminds me of Acts 2:13 when for the first time in the early church, Christians were filled with the Holy Spirit. The manifestation of this experience was so great that mocking observers said, "They are full of new wine." So Hannah was misunderstood as she desperately prayed to her almighty God. Hannah was pouring out her heart to God. Her request for a son was coming from deep within her heart. Earlier in this account of Hannah, it was revealed that her "heart grieved". An emotion of the heart like grieving we can easily understand. We have always been well acquainted with the emotions of the heart. We just do not have the complete understanding of the intellectual properties of the heart. The inner most part of the brain is where the amygdale resides. This part of the brain is considered the emotion eliciting area of the brain. Like many other situations, the heart and brain work together. They work together to express intellect as well as emotion. Hannah soon conceived and bore a son and they named him Samuel. He was a great prophet for God.

> "A good man out of the good treasure of his **heart** brings forth good; and an evil man out of the evil *treasure* of his **heart** brings forth evil, for out of the abundance of the **heart** the mouth *speaks*"
> LUKE 6:45

In the last sentence of this passage, Jesus makes the statement that "out of the abundance of the heart the mouth speaks". This thought pulls together both the speaking and memory aspects of the heart. When I think of "abundance", I contemplate a storehouse of treasures. They may be good treasures or they may be bad. They may be virtuous holdings or corrupt ones. But like an active volcano with a surplus of lava, it eventually breaks forth. We should be very aware of what comes forth from our mouths. What does it reveal about the condition of our heart? The "power of the tongue", which is talked about in the book of James, comes from the heart. We **can** control our tongue, but it becomes possible only when we first learn to "keep" our hearts.

> "Do not be rash with your mouth, and let not your **heart** *utter* anything hastily before God. For God is in heaven; and you earth; therefore let your words be few."
> ECCLESIASTES 5:2

> "When you said, 'seek my face,' my **heart** *said* to You, 'Your face, Lord, I will seek.'" PSALMS 27:8

"Will they not teach you and tell you, and
and *utter* words from their **heart**? JOB 8:10

"An oracle *within* my **heart** concerning the
transgression of the wicked; there is no
fear of God before his eyes."
PSALMS 36:1

Over and over again we see the heart/mouth connection in Scripture. Many times in the book of Ecclesiastes it is expressed, "I said in my *heart.*" The majority of scholars attribute the book of Ecclesiastes to Solomon, the son of David. This book along with the other books of Solomon, Proverbs and The Song of Solomon, contain numerous references of an intelligent heart that communicates. These are statements made by the wisest man on earth. Of course he was under the inspiration of the Holy Spirit. That makes this truth even more profound.

In Psalms 36:1, David, being moved by God, speaks strongly from his heart as revealed by the use of the word "oracle". This word in the original Hebrew is "naham" which is limited to the use of deity. It is almost always translated "saith", and is used in the context of "thus saith the Lord" or "thus saith the Lord God". Being used here by King David emphasizes the idea that his words were given by the inspiration of the Spirit of God. I would contend that this is a significant level of heart maturity. What is happening in these verses is more than David's heart expressing a thought, but rather David's heart is expressing the heart of God. This oracle speaks to the "wicked" having no fear of God in their lives. The apostle Paul writes of this heart condition in Roman 1:21, "because although they (ungodly men) knew God, they did not glorify Him as God, nor were thankful, but became futile in their thoughts, and their foolish **hearts** were darkened". Early in our journey on the road of life we come to a fork in the road. One path provides an awareness of God's existence while the other leads us to a knowledge of God and His righteous ways, eliciting a response of awe and gratitude. If we pick the road which recognizes God, but does not honor Him, the journey ends in a "futile" mind. But if we choose the road David chose; "a man after the heart of God", the trip will result in a heart that understands and expresses the heart of God.

THE HEART TEACHES AND IS TEACHABLE

> "The *heart* of the wise teaches his mouth, and adds *learning* to his lips." PSALMS 16:23

> "...They have a **heart** *trained* in covetous practices, and are accursed children." II PETER 2:14

> "I applied my **heart** to *know*, to seek and search out wisdom and the *reason* of all things..." ECCLESIASTES 7:25

> "For I considered all this in my **heart**, so that I could declare it to all..." ECCLESIASTES 9:1

Like other muscles in our body the heart can be exercised. But I am speaking of a different kind of exercise. The heart's intelligence can be trained to grow in reasoning power and increased wisdom. The heart reaches levels of wisdom where it is capable of "teaching" the mouth and lips what to say. The same heart can also be poorly trained, in "covetous practices". We can choose to "apply" our hearts to know any manner of things; good or bad, enriching or ravaging, thriving or decaying. These choices for the heart can be made in and by the heart.

Let's back up to the first pages of this book. We learned about neurons (brain cells) and how they function. Neurons, we are reminded, form paths by linking up with each other through a process of electromagnetic pulses resulting in a transmission of chemicals from one neuron to other neurons, even thousands of neurons at a time. These pathways, among other things, can create entrenched habits, both good and bad; whether thinking, acting, or feeling. This may best be illustrated by the wagon tracks that were deeply imbedded in the soil on the Oregon Trail. Over one hundred years have passed since then and those ruts are still visible. We are reminded that the heart has neurons as well. The heart's neurons function just like any other neuron, just as brain neurons. Our heart can be trained in right thinking, feeling, and acting or in wrong thinking, feeling, and acting. Taught long enough, and they become habits, either good or bad. With the schooling the heart has received it leads our body or shall I say our soul along the paths it has formed. Yes, the heart is that capable, and is that powerful. The Scripture makes this clear.

THE HEART AND CREATIVITY

> "He has scattered the proud in the imagination of their **heart**.
> LUKE 1:51

These are the words of Mary, the mother of Jesus after Gabriel the angel appeared to her. He declared to her that she had "found favor with God" and in her virgin state would give birth to the Savior of the world. In her declaration of the greatness of God, she makes this statement. What is meant by "imagination of their heart"? I thought the ability to imagine was a function of our minds, not our hearts. This term is found only twice in the King James Version of the New Testament. The other occasion is in Romans 1:21; "...but became vain in their imaginations, and their foolish *heart* was darkened." Note here that it does not say that their mind was "darkened" but rather that their "heart" was darkened. It was foolish imagination of the heart which created damage to the heart. Imagination, is the thinking and feeling of man deliberating within himself with the intent to design or create. Noah Webster, in his first edition of *An American Dictionary of the English Language* defines "imagination" as a conception, an image or idea in the mind. It can be the contrivance, or scheme formed in the mind. But in the context of these Scriptures it is an image, idea, scheme, or contrivance formed in the heart. The heart certainly has creative powers.

> "And I, indeed I, have appointed with him (Bezalel) Aholiab the son of Ahisamach, of the tribe of Dan; and I have put wisdom in the **hearts** of all the *gifted* artisans, that they may make all that I have commanded you."
> Exodus 31:6

In Exodus 31:3 we learn that God had filled Bezalel with

the "Spirit of God, in wisdom, in understanding, in knowledge, and in all manner of workmanship". He gave him the ability to work in all the disciplines of art required to build the tabernacle. For those artists chosen to work with him, God added an extra measure of wisdom in their heart. In Exodus 35:34 we discover that the "ability to teach" was supplied to Aholiab as well. These men were already greatly gifted artisans. But to build something as magnificent as the Tabernacle required an added measure of creativity placed in the heart by God. Unabated gifting was flowing from their hearts. They already possessed the mental gifting of an artist, but were in need of an additional touch of God in their hearts.

> "And Moses said to the children of Israel.
> 'See, the Lord has called by name Bezalel,
> son of Uri, the son, of the tribe of Judah;
> and He has *filled* him with the Spirit of God,
> in *wisdom* and *understanding*, in knowledge
> and all manner of workmanship...And He has
> *put* in his **heart** the ability to teach, in him
> and Aholiab the son of Ahisamach, of the
> tribe of Dan. He has *filled* them with wisdom
> of **heart** to do all manner of work of the
> engraver and the designer and the tapestry
> maker... those who do every work and those
> who design *artistic* works."
> Exodus 35:30-31, 34-35

> Then Moses called Bezalel and Aholiab
> and every gifted *artisan* whose **heart** the
> Lord had put *wisdom,* everyone whose **heart**
> was *stirred* to come and do the work"
> Exodus 36:2

I am not saying that imagination does not take place in the mind; it certainly does. But I am asserting that it is also a function of the heart. I am convinced that when the mind and the heart are in sync, our greatest accomplishments are realized. In the past when I thought of a wise person I was limiting my understanding to intellectual pursuits. I did not link wisdom and manual skills together, nor associate artistic talent with wisdom. But God places a great deal of importance on manual and artistic endeavors. The wisest man you know may be the person who painted your portrait or laid the brick for your fireplace. One of our children is a gifted artist. His mother and I became aware of his talent when he was very young. Over the years his talent developed as he spent extra time each day drawing. As he continued to embrace this gift, God continued to bless his talent. Today he is a professional artist, greatly benefitting from God's work in his heart and mind.

We also learn that God put into the heart of Bezalel and Aholiab the ability to teach these skills. The Tabernacle was an extraordinary assignment that required a great number of skilled artisans. And to be successful, these artisans would need far more than their natural gifting. This extra wisdom for the heart was taught by other men whose hearts were prepared for the task. But, for it all to come together, the artisans and additional workers would need motivation. That too was supplied from those whose hearts were "stirred". Again we see the encompassing greatness of the heart. At this important occasion in biblical history, the success of the endeavor was realized by the heart of men, taught from the heart of men, and enriched by the heart of God.

As I shared in the beginning, this chapter was intended to

provide an overview of the vastness of the heart of man as recorded in Scripture. In subsequent chapters I will go into far more detail, relying on significant amounts of Scripture. The goal will be to uncover further truths of the heart that will not only enrich our lives, but give us life. The final authority, of course, will continue to be the Word of God.

Ponder this in your Heart

Contemplate the amazing attributes of the heart that in the past you may have only credited to the mind and list the ways this might influence your daily life.

CHAPTER THREE | Guard Your Heart

"Keep your heart with all diligence for out of it spring the issues of life."
Proverbs 4:23

Wow! This Scripture is a real mouthful. Or should I say a heart full? Read it slowly with your heart, focusing on each individual word. This entire study centers on this verse. All the principles that we gain from the Scriptures concerning the heart revolve around the truths found in this verse. It is as if we were constructing an old fashioned wooden wagon wheel with spokes extending from the hub. Proverbs 4:23 is the hub around which additional Scripture references will revolve. Like the hub of a wheel, our heart is at the center of what moves us down the road of life. The health of our physical, emotional, intellectual, and spiritual heart will determine how successfully this road is traveled. Let's take a closer look at this verse.

As mentioned earlier the Hebrew word for heart in the Old Testament is "lehv". In the New Testament the Greek word for heart is "kardia". From this term we derive the English word "cardiac", which refers to all things pertaining to the heart. Cardiac arrest is a level of heart failure. A Cardiologist is a heart specialist. "Heart" itself means center, or taking central place. Heart is at the center, and is central. Physically it is in the center of our body. It is central to living healthy. The same is true of our spiritual heart. In fact, if our spiritual heart is out of balance then our physical heart will struggle as well. The two are more closely connected than we can imagine. For example, statistically, men who have anger issues are twice as likely to have a heart attack. Stress has a profound weakening affect upon the heart. Stress has much to do with fear and anxiety; which along with anger, are spiritual issues dealt with in the Bible. Centuries ago, physicians recognized the connection between the mind and the body. In recent decades they have drifted back to that understanding. But now, science is going even deeper and beginning to acknowledge a connection between the spiritual heart and physical health. I think we would all agree that a strong physical heart is essential for a healthy body.

We are admonished to "keep" our heart. I am sure this could be approached from both a physiological or spiritual perspective. If we are going to obey this command we must first clearly understand the meaning of "keep". The root Hebrew word is "nahzar" which conveys the understanding of watching over something, and also to guard and observe. Psalms 141:3 declares; "Set a guard, O Lord, over my mouth; keep watch over the door of my lips." Added meaning would be "to keep a vineyard". We are to go beyond just paying attention to our heart. The instruction is to keep it, as a farmer would keep his vineyard. He would care for his vineyard in such a manner as to keep it healthy, and carry it through each level to maturity, at which point the vineyard would yield fruit, hopefully a bountiful crop.

In this verse, "keep" is used in the imperative sense. This means that the action is now, immediate, and mandatory. This is not a negotiable item with God. But obedience will bring tremendous fruit in our lives. "Nazhar" also conveys the understanding of being verdant, that is to flourish and advance in strength. God declares that it is imperative that our hearts grow and flourish as a green plant. Our hearts are not to remain status quo and certainly not regress. No matter what age, we do not need to become complacent. We can have a growing heart brimming with vitality. I am convinced by Scripture that a healthy spiritual heart will stimulate health for our physical hearts as well. The word "keep" is also used in Proverbs 3:1. "My son do not forget my law, but let your *heart* keep my commands." In order for the Word of God to flourish in our lives it must be guarded and cultivated. It must be nourished in our hearts so life may flow forth.

This is serious business! We are instructed to approach this task with all diligence. Not a little effort, but with total effort and purpose. "All", meaning everything, nothing left over. "Diligent" in its root understanding means that this endeavor is the most important of all. It is also used in Scripture as "ward"; with the understanding that we are a "guardian" of our heart. A guardian performs his responsibility constantly, day and night. We are to exercise the utmost vigilance, as if we are building a fortress around our heart, with guard posts that are manned at all times. This may seem like an impossible task, but I assure you it is not. The heart is more than willing to assist in this task and God has supplied all the tools needed. It must be clear how important the heart is to God.

There are a number of ways that different Bible translators express "spring the issues of life", and they are all helpful. For example: "flow the springs", "are the issues", and "springs life". When distilled down to its core, the meaning is; the heart is life! We have the strongest available motivation now for being energized to do God's will, and follow this command. We understand that the heart *is our life*! I am not discounting the truth that Christ is our life. Christ by His Spirit lives out His life in our Heart. "And because you are sons, God has sent forth the Spirit of His Son into your *hearts* crying out, 'Abba Father!'" (Galatians 4:6). There are numerous Scripture that declare this truth; "Christ in you the hope of Glory." Colossians 1:27. For now let it suffice to say that our heart is of utmost importance. Why? Because God declares it to be, and gives us hundreds of Scripture to teach us its truth.

The word "issues" in this passage could just as easily been translated, "fountains". Our heart gushes forth with fountains of life. This speaks to the intensity of life within us. Our heart is like a new oil well, bursting forth with black gold. It leaves the ground with incredible power and takes great skill and strength to control its flow. The heart is intelligent, and controlling the flow is inherent, when it is in God's keeping. This bursting forth of life from our inner being was declared by Jesus. "He who believes in me as the Scripture said, 'From his innermost being shall flow rivers of living water.' But this He spoke of the Spirit, whom those who believed in Him were to receive; for the Spirit was not yet given, because Jesus was not yet glorified." (John 7:38-39 NASV). This in all its glory brings us to an important fact. We are the subject of this verse!

In elementary and junior high I had a tremendous English teacher. Mrs. Marsh was a very godly woman with tremendous teaching skills. Her two greatest attributes were that she loved God and loved us, her students. She was the first to teach me how to diagram sentences and I wish I fully remembered all the nuances of this art. As I recall a portion of this procedure I am reminded that the reader is the subject of this verse. "You" is the understood subject, "guard" is the verb, and "heart" is the object. This instruction from God directly involves each one of us. We must take this admonition very personally. Don't be over concerned about someone else's heart that you see is in need of repair. First take inventory of your own heart. This does not preclude that you have a wicked heart in great need, but rather you may have simply overlooked a wonderful opportunity to enrich your life. Let's take a look at some additional Scriptures that will surely enrich our hearts.

The Proverbs of the Old Testament were written by God through the pen of Solomon, the wisest man on earth. The first verses of Proverbs declare its purpose. "To know wisdom and instruction, to perceive the words of understanding, to receive the instruction of wisdom, justice, judgment, and equity; to give prudence to the simple, to the young man knowledge and discretion" (Proverbs 1:2-4). The word 'heart' is used nearly one hundred times in Proverbs; over three times per chapter. When it comes to wisdom, knowledge, and understanding, the heart must be the key.

> *"My son, if you receive my words, and treasure my commands within you, so that you incline your ear to wisdom, and apply your **heart** to understanding; yes, if you cry out for discernment, and lift up your voice for understanding, if you seek her as silver, and search for her as for hidden treasures; then you will understand the fear of the Lord, and find the knowledge of God."* PROVERBS 2:1-5

The first step of obtaining wisdom is to understand the fear of the Lord. Most Christians have been taught this truth, but could it be possible, that in many cases an important element was left out? We need to go beyond a mental understanding, to a deeper level by burying this truth deep in our hearts. To fear God is to see Him as He is: mighty and powerful in all His glory. In Noah Webster's 1828 Dictionary, he defines the fear of God as a "holy awe or reverence of God and His laws, which springs from a just view and real love of the divine character, leading the subjects of it to hate and shun everything that can offend such a holy being, and inclining them to aim at perfect obedience". I am convinced that this high calling of "fearing God" can only become real in our lives by engaging our hearts. This must be a truth received into our hearts and acted upon from our hearts. God declares through His prophet Jeremiah that "I will put my fear in their hearts". According to King Solomon this is where it all begins. The first step in gaining knowledge and wisdom, even the knowledge of God, is to "apply our hearts to knowledge". As we know, there are numerous references in Proverbs concerning the heart. Let's look at a few of them.

> "A sound **heart** is *life* to the body…"
> PROVERBS 14:30

> "When wisdom enters your **heart**, and
> knowledge is pleasant to your soul,
> discretion will preserve you;
> understanding will *keep* you."
> PROVERBS 2:10-11

Our body and soul are both discussed in these Scriptures. If we desire a strong body, body building may not be the only path we pursue. In fact, it is likely not the best first choice. Allow me to list several words that make up the qualities of a "sound heart": unbroken, undecayed, perfect, whole, entire, unhurt, unmutilated, healthy, complete, firm, solid; and the list goes on and on. A healthy heart will bring health to the entire body. A healthy spiritual heart will bring health to our physical heart. God is in the business of healing broken hearts. Our hearts are more vulnerable than we think. But that is not the case when they are built up by the Word of God. We understand from these verses that when wisdom enters our heart (not our mind), it brings pleasure to our souls. If you really want to please your "self", that is your soul, then reach for your Bible and feed your heart.

> "My son do not forget my law, but let your **heart** keep my commands; for length of days and long *life* and peace they will *add* to you."
> PROVERBS 3:1-2

Repeatedly we see the importance of the heart and why it is critical to keep a watch over it. It is the source of an enriched and thriving life; emotionally, physically, and spiritually. God's law is to be kept in and by the heart. It is not a total exercise of the mind. It is not just a mental pursuit. I believe that the heart has the capacity to keep God's commandments where the mind struggles. Do not misunderstand me. I am not saying that the Law saves us; Christ alone saves by His shed blood. But I am repeating what God says in His word, that our heart is to keep his commands. The word "keep" is the same word used in Proverbs 4:23; the pivotal verse on guarding the heart.

Keeping God's law in your heart promises many significant benefits. We will enjoy fuller days, more days to our life, and wonderful peace. In the middle of my research on the heart, I fell into a life-threatening illness. I was not expected to survive the surgery; my condition had advanced too far. I did come out of the surgery, but the road back to health has been painfully slow. Several months later I was back in the hospital four times in one month. Much of that time I was unconscious. There have been several therapies in my regiment for total healing, Bible meditation being the most important. Thanks to my family's endurance, the Scriptures were read to me for hours in the hospital. No matter my state of consciousness, this practice continued. When I arrived home an electronic tablet was sitting next to my chair with the Bible downloaded on it. My family made sure it was playing nearly all day long. I took the Scriptures into my heart every day for months. I went through the Bible many times, and I continue doing so today. I can personally contest to the power of God's word in my heart. I know my heart has been enlarged, my body strengthened, and my soul nourished. As strange as it may seem, the days seem to last longer. That is not because I am sitting home bored all day. I am out and around now, enjoying many different activities. I have even gone out of state on a mini vacation. My heart and I have made a lot of progress together. The amount of peace that God has planted in my heart is above explanation. It's amazing! The peace I enjoy daily is far more than I ever thought possible.

> "Wisdom *resteth* in the **heart** of him that hath understanding: but that which is in the midst of fools is made known.
> PROVERBS 14:33 KJV

Throughout Proverbs, Solomon contrasts the foolish person and the wise person. The condition they find themselves in is due to the contents of their heart. Wisdom rests in the Heart of a man with understanding. The root meaning of "resteth" is what you would imagine—to rest. The Bible often admonishes us to rest in the Lord. Then of course, there is our eternal heavenly rest. Rest means to be quiet, to lie or set down. To put something to rest means to deposit it for safe keeping with intent that it remains there. When God promises rest He is offering seclusion, privacy and peace. This is what the believer experiences with God's wisdom in his heart. Wisdom has been deposited for safe keeping, in the center of his being.

Not so for the fool. He has entirely different contents in the midst of his being. There is a lack of privacy, security, or peace. Everything is "made known". No secrets - "the cat is out of the bag". In modern vernacular - "it is all over Facebook". The contents of a fool's heart often include anger. "Be not hasty in thy spirit to be angry: for anger resteth in the bosom of fools" (Ecclesiastes 7:9 KJV). It certainly is not wise to be angry. There is a difference between a man who is capable of getting angry, and an angry man. In the angry man the anger resides; it takes up residence. Anger cannot reside in a wise heart; they cannot coexist. It is not that we do not have to deal with anger; it can come and go. But wisdom will not allow it to stay. God's gift to our heart is not anger, but rather peace, the peace you experience when resting.

> "As in water face reflects face, so a man's
> **heart** *reveals* the man."
> Proverbs 27:19

This Scripture does not require a word study. The meaning is quite clear. It is as clear as your refection in the mirror. This is one of the strongest references to the heart in all the Scriptures. I will often go on in conversation for extended periods of time, trying to make a point clear. Then in one simple sentence or two, only taking a minute, my wife will sum up everything I rambled on about. This proverb does just that, it sums up everything about the heart.

In the summer we try to enjoy as much time as possible at the family cabin on the lake. If I get up really early in the morning, which frankly interferes with my rest, I will find a lake as smooth as glass. In my youth, that was the perfect time to go for a ski ride. It was nearly as clear as looking at myself in the mirror, even if I did not like what I saw. The heart reveals a true and accurate picture of who we are. When we look in a mirror we have the confidence of knowing that we are looking at ourselves. We have always trusted the mirror to be one hundred percent accurate in reflecting our appearance. We may want to change what we see, but the mirror does not have the ability to do that. But the heart does have that ability. If you receive a new heart, you become a new man. The heart is the perfect gauge of who you are. God works on and through our heart to make changes that last forever. God knows our heart, and he can make our hearts known, both to ourselves and others. When God changes the heart of a man, He changes the man. This will become even clearer as we study additional verses about the heart

> "Do not let your adornment be merely outward—arranging the hair, wearing

> gold or putting on fine apparel—rather
> let it be the *hidden person* of the **heart**,
> with the incorruptible beauty of a gentle
> and quiet spirit, which is very precious
> in the sight of God. I Peter 3:34

The context of this passage is Peter encouraging women to do more than just focus on their outward appearance. I remember a famous preacher saying on more than one occasion, "if the barn needs painting, then paint it". He said this in a kind and humorous manner, which by no means was offensive to women. There is nothing wrong with looking the best we possibly can. We really should put our best foot forward. But let's not miss the purpose of these verses. Peter is emphasizing the difference between outer and inner beauty. Our top priority should be the "hidden person". The Greek word used here for "hidden", is found three other times in the New Testament. In each of these verses the intention is to bring the object out of hiding. In Revelation 2:17, Christ promises the overcomers at the Church of Pergamos that they will eat of the hidden manna. But remember we are addressing "the hidden person of the *heart*". We see this same context in I Corinthians 4:5 when Paul reminds the Corinthian Church that when the Lord comes He will "bring to light the hidden things of darkness and reveal the counsels of the hearts".

What does it mean, the "counsels" of the heart? Are we talking about the counsel we might receive in a therapy session? Are we speaking of a "heart to heart" conversation between loved ones? In our vernacular a more accurate term to use would be the "contents" of our heart. And add to that the purpose of those contents as they speak to

God's divine plan. Our hearts are to declare the wonderful works of God by being "adorned" with "incorruptible beauty". Our outward person is certainly corrupted by the ravages of time. But there are those people whose hidden beauty is made known to all, and it far outweighs the loss of fleeting outward beauty. These people "shine" right into and through their later years. And I do mean "shine" because the Greek word used for "adornment" is "kosmos" used often in Scripture to speak of God's creation, the world. Christ, in the Sermon on the Mount declared that we are the "light of the world". Paul in his letter to the Philippians admonished them to "shine as lights in the world". When we decorate our bodies with jewelry, we are hanging on ornaments. When God does a work in our inner person, He is infusing our hearts with "a gentle and quiet spirit". And these qualities are "incorruptible". They are eternal, and cannot be tarnished or even destroyed.

This is a powerful Scripture. It would be wise if we set aside a period of time to really meditate upon its meaning. We all have a hidden person that God wants revealed to others. The abode of this person, with the gentle and quiet spirit, is their heart. This is who you are, as a spiritual man or woman. Your heart reveals who you really are, and God takes pleasure in the heart of a person with a gentle and quiet spirit. Many of us would not describe ourselves as being gentle and calm. And perhaps we are accurate in that assessment. But have we been struggling with our mental intellect to bring this to pass? If so, then we have taken the wrong approach. This is a work God does in the heart, not in the brain. Engage your heart, and allow it to cooperate with God's work in your inner being. Then shine like a star!

> "But take heed to yourselves lest your
> **hearts** be *weighed* down with carousing,
> drunkenness, and the cares of life, and that
> Day come on you unexpectedly."
> LUKE 21:34

These next Scripture texts are chosen to transition us into the following chapter. We are right back from where we started. We are to be alert to the condition of our heart. We are to "take heed" lest it go in the wrong direction. There are many things that can damage our hearts, and Christ mentions some critical ones here. We use the phrase "being light hearted". By this we mean care free, perhaps without a worry. The opposite would be a heart "weighed down" with the cares of the world. Many go to "drink" in the attempt to remain light hearted, but just the opposite happens. Or others will escape the drudgery of life by carousing with their friends and the result again is a heart weighed down, a heavy heart. This can become habitual, a way of life. If this is our state, then God warns that the "Day" will catch us off guard. Christ describes that "Day" when He declares: "Heaven and earth will pass away, but My words will by no means pass away". Planting God's word in our heart and making friends with those who live by the same ideals will prepare us for heaven. The meaning of these Scriptures is equally expressed in Proverbs 23:17: "Do not let your heart envy sinners, but be zealous for the fear of the Lord all the day".

> "Do not eat the bread of a miser,
> nor desire his delicacies, for as he
> *thinks* in his **heart,** so is he. Eat and
> drink he says to you, but his **heart** is
> not with you." The morsel you have

> eaten, you will vomit up, and waste your pleasant words."
> PROVERBS 23:6-8

The proper sort of friends is essential to Godly living. It is not easy at first, to evaluate the character of a potential friend. But if we allow our hearts the time to scrutinize our position with other people, we will learn the art of "discernment". I am not talking about placing judgment on others; that is being judgmental. No, rather I am saying we need to make right judgments; we must be wise. In this example, we need to be wise of heart. As the Proverbs reveal, real wisdom comes from the heart, and a healthy one at that.

We are encouraged to avoid a person who is a miser. The King James Version of the Bible gives us a clearer understanding. It says, "Him that hath an evil eye". The emphasis is on "evil". The word "noxious" has been used to interpret the Hebrew word for evil. That is a very appropriate term for the experience we have from bad food. The context of this passage goes beyond food, implying that the time we spend with an evil hearted person may very well make us sick. We should desire the aptitude of discernment that the Lord possessed. This is made clear in Luke 9:47. "And Jesus perceiving the thought of their *heart*, took a little child and set him by them". This passage reminds us again that the heart thinks. Our heart can think good or bad things, likewise our friends. We, like Jesus, can learn to discern the condition of a heart, but first our heart must be one with Christ's. Later in the book this point will be clearly proved by Scripture. It should be noted that when Jesus perceived hearts that were lacking, He turned His attention to a child. We could probably learn a great deal by studying the heart of a child. But for now we need to look in depth at the condition of a heart that would render it untrustworthy.

Ponder this in your Heart

Stop and reflect on the importance of guarding your heart. Pray to God, asking for His grace to make this truth a reality in your life.

CHAPTER FOUR | An Unreliable Heart

> "And God saw that the wickedness of man was great in the earth and that every *imagination* of the thoughts of his **heart** was evil continually." And the Lord was sorry that He had made man on the earth, and was grieved in His **heart**."
> GENESIS 6:5-6

I was having a conversation one day with a dear friend about some of the intricacies of the heart. He asked me this very basic but profound question. When do we become aware that we are thinking with our hearts? This question immediately reminded me of Piaget's Stages of Cognitive Development. Jean Piaget spent half a century studying the mental development of children. He pulled together four basic stages covering birth to twelve years of age. The third stage, "concrete operational" marks the point when children begin to know that they are thinking, and that they have control in its processes. They begin to venture out, using their brain to grasp concrete events and to form thoughts. My answer to his question was as follows: "I do not think it works the same with the heart as it does with the brain."

My view is that it is not a question of when we first realized that our heart started to think and direct us, but when did our heart STOP thinking. As mentioned earlier, the physical heart is beating before the brain is even formed. It is doing its job well in advance of other bodily organs. The heart can survive after being disconnected from the brain. Our heart was doing a great job of thinking long before we realized our control over thought patterns. Some of us may want to ask the following questions. What has happened in my life to inhibit my heart from being in true form? When was it that I quit listening to my heart? When did purity of heart cease from being a priority? The answer is not exactly the same for everyone. None the less we all need to be acutely aware of the condition of our heart.

There may not be a need to engage our hearts, but instead get something out of the way so it can work efficiently. I live in a part of the country that has many artesian wells. Artesian wells are underground streams that flow continuously year round. When I was a child many of these streams were close to the surface of the earth. But even under these ideal conditions the flow of water could be easily thwarted. Imagine an old hand pump that just won't bring forth the water no matter how heartily you pump. After closer examination an old dirty rag is discovered lodged in the pipe when it is removed the life giving water flows.

Years ago we bought a home for our family on a small acreage. This home was in the country and had its own artesian well, and its own septic system. In order for our house to function properly it was essential that the sewage in the tank flowed efficiently. Well, the day came when this was not the case. Unfortunately the sewage was backing up into the house. I immediately contacted someone to pump out the tank. He pumped it out three times but the tank continued to fill up. It would not empty itself. It just did not make any sense. So I did the smart thing. I prayed! God led me to find and study the diagram which

An Unreliable Heart

detailed the layout of the septic system. Several feet underground there was a valve in the pipe between the tank and the drain field. There was very little sewage flowing through this sleeve and when I turned it an additional hole opened up and the waste streamed through. I know this is a distasteful illustration—but it is true, and very helpful. God had answered my prayer and our house was protected from harm and restored to us again as a proper dwelling. If you have discovered that your heart is not functioning correctly, perhaps you should cry out to God and ask Him to remove from your life that which is blocking your heart and inhibiting its flow of life.

The Genesis passage we started this chapter with is the first time that the word "heart" is used. In studying the Bible it is important to note the first time that God addresses a subject, as well as the last occasion. In these verses when God made it clear that He was displeased with man, He did not address the condition of his mind. God focused on the heart. And not just on the heart itself, but its processes. The wickedness of man was out of control and God did not begin by addressing his deeds, but went to the root and dealt with man's heart. God declared that man's heart was evil. God goes into detail and in doing so teaches us much about the human heart. The "thoughts" of the heart were evil. Yes, again we see that the heart thinks. But it does not always think properly. Even in the issues of the heart we have free will. We have input into the ultimate condition of our heart. The Scripture goes into more detail when it states that the "imaginations" of the thoughts of the heart were evil, and adds that they were evil "continually".

What does this all mean? This great wickedness on earth was man's doing and had its source in his heart. It was birthed in the imagination of his heart. Note that God did not say the imagination of his mind. Yes, the heart thinks as the brain thinks and it imagines as the brain imagines. Scripture makes clear what science is now discovering. The heart literally has imagination, one of many qualities and attributes of thinking. Man had fallen to the point that from the first thought when he woke (and perhaps even in his sleep), to the final thought on his pillow, all his thinking was evil. Boiled down, the original Hebrew language says, "every thought of the thoughts" was wicked and evil. The conception and formation of the thoughts were evil. The creating and forming a plan or scheme was evil. And the conclusion was wicked deeds that went on continually.

In order to desire and really appreciate a good and powerful heart we need to clearly understand its evil potential. If we are truly going to see a need to be rescued, we must first realize we are perishing. A drowning man will yell for help when he is aware that the crashing waves will soon suffocate him. You may not be aware that the roof of your house is in flames until someone knocks on your door and makes you aware. This chapter contains many Scriptures that are not exactly on the warm and fuzzy side. God destroyed the world with a flood because of the condition of man's heart. Why do we want to be reminded of that? The answer is clear. Like Noah, God always gives us a way of escape. He desires to change an evil heart to a good heart. And that is exactly what we see Him doing in Scripture and in the lives of His children today.

This passage in Genesis of course is the story of the world wide flood. It not only is the first place that man's heart is mentioned, but also the first occasion for the mentioning of God's Heart. God was sorry that He had made man. We

An Unreliable Heart

have always been aware of the emotions of the heart. It is this thinking aspect that catches us off guard. But God's emotions are paramount here. He is not flying off the handle in response to His out-of-control children. He is about to remove all of His creation from the face of the earth, except for Noah and his family. This thought alone "grieved His *heart*". As Scripture teaches "we are made in the image of God". God has emotions and we have emotions. God has a heart and we have a heart. "God is Spirit, and those who worship Him, must worship Him in Spirit and truth" (John 4:24). And the truth here is that God was greatly grieved in his heart. It hurt him very deeply. His decision was not preceded by calculated scheming, but by a broken heart of compassion. Grief is a strong emotion, one well experienced by those who have lost a loved one. That is exactly the point. God lost all but a very few of His beloved children. When it was over and done, He set a new direction for the state of His creation.

> "Then the Lord said in His **heart,** ' I will never again curse the ground for man's sake although the *imagination* of man's **heart** is *evil* from his youth; nor will I again destroy every living thing as I have done." GENESIS 8:21

God's heart never changes. His heart is continually perfect and pure, without blemish, and full of love. Man's heart is quite the opposite and God does not wait for man to respond before He sets His course. God said "in His *heart*" that He would never curse the ground again for the benefit of man, even though man's heart remained evil. He vowed to Himself that He would never again destroy every living thing as He had done in the flood. And remember, this was His creation that He deeply loved. The loss had caused Him great grief. The evil character of man has no influence on the holy character of God. Christ made it clear in The Sermon on the Mount that God continues to make "His sun rise on the evil and on the good, and sends rain on the just and on the unjust" (Matthew 5:45).

> "The fool has said in his **heart**, 'there is no God.' They are corrupt, and have done abominable iniquity; there is none who does good." PSALMS 53:1

No one wants to be called a fool, yet that is exactly what God does when addressing anyone who has no place for Him in his heart. Let me remind you what God did not say. He did not say "The fool has said in his *mind*." Our minds are perplexed and overwhelmed by many things, constantly searching for truth. It is an extraordinary endeavor for the human mind to contemplate the universe. It comes much easier for the heart, for God declares that He "has put eternity in their (man's) *heart*" (Ecclesiastes 2:20). If we allow ourselves to decline to the point that we deny God in our hearts, then we have stepped on a downward spiraling slide. It is a path that leads to "abominable iniquity". It leads to a life that can do no good, and even worse, is continually bent on a course of hateful, detestable, and loathsome behavior. To make it very clear—a man whose heart will not acknowledge God and has reconciled himself to living like a depraved criminal with no interest in extending justice to others, that is a heart you cannot trust.

> "But the Lord said to Samuel. 'Do not look at his appearance or at his physical stature, because I have refused him. For the Lord does not see as man sees; for a man *looks* at the outward appearance, but the Lord *looks* at the **heart**." I Samuel 16:7

It is inevitable that our first inclination is to measure a person by their outward appearance. If this does not come naturally then we are certainly taught so on a continuing basis. Outward beauty is paramount in our culture, as well as many others. The generation I belong to, the "baby boomers", are doing everything possible to keep from looking older. I am not saying this is wrong, but our methods may be out of whack. We are working from the outside in, instead of from the inside out. The outward appearance is simply a reflection of the *heart*; "For as he (man) thinks in his heart, so is he" (Proverbs 23:7).

The context of I Samuel 16:7 was Samuel choosing a king to replace Saul. Saul had disobeyed God and as a result God had "rejected him from reigning over Israel". Samuel was "mourning over Saul" when God instructed him to go to Jesse and pick one of his sons as the new king. Samuel was not lacking when it came to spiritual maturity, yet he was vulnerable to the same inclination as all of us, focusing on the visual attributes. Saul was handsome, and stood head and shoulders above other men. I suspect that Samuel was looking for another imposing figure. One by one Jesse paraded his sons in front of Saul; starting with Eliab, then Abinadab, then Shammah, and then the final four. But God refused them all. There was still one son left, out tending the sheep. Ironically though, he was also a man of attractive appearance; being "ruddy, with bright eyes, and good looking". But we discover an additional attribute when God says that he was "a man after My own *heart*, who will do all My will". David had the added inner beauty of a heart aimed at pleasing God.

Frequently in my life I have made the mistake of evaluating the potential of a person based on visible attributes. I am not just referring to physical attractiveness. I have been drawn by an outgoing personality, a witty disposition, a quick intellect, all of which fall short when not backed up by a mature heart. Like it was yesterday, I can remember sitting in the balcony during a church service admiring an attractive family lined up in a pew below me. All seemed well, dressed handsomely, not a smug look of rebellion or haughtiness. But as the Scripture points out, "...be sure your sins will find you out" (Numbers 32:23), proved true. Over a short period of time the entire family washed out in their walk with Christ. That was many years ago and I am not aware of their current condition. But I do hope that the healing that comes with a HEART sold out to God is their cherished possession.

The heart that cannot be trusted is clearly seen in the life of Pharaoh. I am speaking of the Pharaoh of Exodus who was extremely reluctant to release the children of Israel. Twenty times from Exodus chapter four to fourteen God comments on the "hardness" of Pharaoh's heart. God does not describe Pharaoh as a "hard-headed" man; but rather a "hard-hearted" man. There certainly is no denying that he was hard headed. It took ten torturing plagues to change his mind. He finally allowed the people of Israel, under Moses' leadership to leave. But his hard heart ultimately ruled over his mind leading him to chase after Israel and causing the destruction of his own army. God uses the term "hard-hearted" throughout the entire Bible helping us to comprehend the heart condition that will surely bring destruction. God desires that we possess a heart that will bring life.

> "If I regard iniquity in my **heart** the Lord will not hear." Psalms **66:18**

What is iniquity? How does it differ from sin? Iniquity is not a synonym for sin, but it certainly is a sin. It is a grievous sin. We do not want it in our heart. It fosters injustice, wickedness, and crime. We can fully understand iniquity by knowing its opposite. "Rectitude", the opposing trait, sums up all that is right and correct, exact conformity to truth. An absence of righteousness adequately defines "iniquity". In Scripture, the prophet Isaiah says that our iniquities separate us from God. A heart with iniquity can only be expected to lead us away from God. It will never allow the light of God to shine in our hearts. It keeps God from hearing our prayers, from answering our pleas. It will only keep us from God's saving grace. That is death, not life.

What Does Jesus Say

I have made a point to cover all areas of the Bible concerning the possible conditions of our heart, and the most important view point is that of Jesus Christ. He spoke often on the Heart and its central place in our spiritual, emotional, and intellectual endeavors. He spoke intensely, plainly, and powerfully so that there would be no mistake on its importance. I have chosen just a few of those occasions, but enough to thoroughly cover God's heart on the topic, expressed through His son.

> "But Jesus knowing their thoughts, said, 'why do you *think* evil in your **hearts**?'"
> MATTHEW 9:4

> "A good man out of the good treasure of his **heart** brings forth good things, and an evil man out of the evil treasure brings forth evil things. For out of the *abundance* of the **heart** his mouth *speaks*." LUKE 6:45

Jesus knows our thoughts and the type of thinking that matters to Him the most is that which comes from the heart. Jesus clearly proclaims that the heart thinks, and it is imperative that these thoughts are moral. Luke's recording uses the term "treasure" in describing the contents of the heart. And let's not forget that Jesus is not talking about the heart in general, but He is specifically talking about "his" (our personal) heart. We store up memories, ideas, and dreams in our heart. This storehouse is so valuable that God refers to it as a "treasure". I imagine that most of us have believed that treasures as a rule are very valuable, very good. But Christ makes it clear that some treasure can be bad and therefore harmful to ourselves and others. Christ does not mince words when He says evil things flow from the hearts of evil men. And good things flow from the hearts of good men. The heart and the man are inseparable. And that heart is abundantly full, brimming over, flowing freely with life giving or life destroying power. The choice is ours; and the choice we make proclaims loudly who we are; either good or evil

> "Brood of vipers! How can you, being evil speak good things? For out of the abundance of the **heart** the mouth speaks. The good man out of the good treasure of his **heart** *brings forth* good things, and the evil man out of the evil treasure *brings forth* evil things. But I say to you that for every idle word men may speak, they will give account of it in the day of judgment. For by your words you will be justified, and by your words you will be condemned." MATTHEW 12:34-37

The accounts of Luke and Matthew are quite similar in their recording of Christ's assessment of the human heart. But Matthew begins with a very harsh description of those driven by an evil heart. Christ calls them vipers, a rather detestable and loathing snake, capable of poisoning its prey, bringing about certain death. Proverbs 18:21 informs us that "Death and life are in the power of the tongue". Whoever coined the term, "sticks and stones can break my bones, but words will never harm me", could not have been further from the truth. Words have tremendous power. We have the privilege of commanding either a blessing or a curse. These are born in a powerful heart. Our words, proceeding from our heart, bring either life or death. The nature of the words we speak and the condition of our heart are one and the same. Sooner or later your mouth is going to give you away; probably sooner than later. James 3:8-9 says that "No man can tame the tongue, it is an unruly evil, full of deadly poison. With it we bless our God and Father, and with it we curse men, who have been made in the likeness of God." No, we cannot not tame the tongue, but we can tame the heart, which has power over the tongue. As we continue on in our study of the heart, that fact will become crystal clear.

> "For the **hearts** of this people have grown *dull*. Their ears are hard of hearing, and their eyes they have closed, lest they should see with their eyes and hear with their ears, lest they should *understand* with their **hearts** and turn, so that I should heal them." MATTHEW 13:15

Here Jesus quotes the prophet Isaiah. We are well aware of the term "dull-witted" which is used to describe a slow thinking person. But we may not equate this quality to a potential condition of our heart. The greater problem is not a dull mind, but rather a dull heart. When our hearts grow dull other senses in our body follow suit, and in turn when our senses are misused a dull heart results. But as we will focus on later, a proper use of our senses will "guard" our hearts. But when we become hard of hearing and seeing, we become blind to the truth that can set us free. A heart bent on pleasing God will experience the healing that only God can provide. A heart bent on evil will spiral down and down into even greater destruction. This fact is clearly revealed by Matthew 15:18-19. "But those things which proceed out of the mouth come from the *heart* and they defile a man. For out of the *heart* proceed evil thoughts, murders, adulteries, fornications, thefts, false witness, and blasphemies." Let us be clear on what it means to be defiled. It is the corruption of morals, principles, and character; becoming dirty, foul, polluted, and corrupted. This obviously is not a good place to be. Thank God that he can give us a new heart, and He greatly desires to do so.

> "...Why do you reason because you have no bread? Do you not yet perceive nor understand? Is your **heart** still *hardened?*"
> MARK 8:17

> "Because of the hardness of your **heart** he wrote you this precept." MARK 10:5

> "Later He appeared to the eleven as they sat at the table; and He rebuked their *unbelief* and *hardness* of **heart**, because they did not believe those who had seen Him after He had risen." MARK 16:14

"Hardness of Heart" which over and over again describes the heart of pharaoh in the Book of Exodus, can easily be our fate as well. At this point some may say that I am being too harsh by laboring on the point of how corrupt man's heart is capable of becoming. But it is not me. I am simply sharing what Christ him-self made abundantly clear in His teaching. He wants us to know just how lost we are until we are found by Him. We are that one "lost sheep" that He the shepherd is diligent, at all costs, to find and save. It is "hardness" of heart that mocks the testimony of others sharing how God's loving grace has been poured out in their life. It is "hardness" of heart that brushes away the loving hand of God placed gently on our shoulder. It is "hardness" of heart that finds no place to kneel in prayer or to shout "thank you" to our heavenly father for His abundant generosity.

The prophet Hosea preached, "...break up the fallow

ground, for it is time to seek the Lord, till He comes and rains righteousness on you" (Hosea 10:12). The prophet Jeremiah makes the same admonition. They were urging God's chosen people who had turned their backs on God to get their hearts right toward Him. They had become a "hard-hearted" people who needed to be softened. Perhaps who still remember how a field is prepared for planting. If it has remained fallow, neglected and uncultivated, for a period of time it must be plowed up or softened to receive the planted seed. Our hearts must also be softened, readied to receive the Word of God. When that seed in the heart matures, it will burst forth and produce fruit a hundred fold or more. Our hearts are the place of our greatest productivity if we will allow Christ to do His great work there.

Satan's Access to the Heart

For decades a very serious subject has been bantered back and forth among Christians. The imposing argument seeks to answer whether or not a Christian can be possessed by a demon. This is very important business, yet, I am not convinced we are asking the best question. I have chosen to study the Scriptures concerning Satan's access to our soul. I especially want to focus on His potential influence on our heart. Does Satan have access to our heart?

> "Jesus answered them, 'did I not choose you, the twelve, and one of you is a devil?' He spoke of Judas Iscariot, the son of Simon, for it was he who would *betray H*im, being one of the twelve." JOHN 6:70-71

An Unreliable Heart

Early in His ministry with the twelve disciples Jesus spoke these very poignant words. Well in advance He was prophesying the state of Judas' soul at the time when Christ would be coming to the close of His earthly ministry. Judas was there with all the disciples to experience firsthand the wonderful works of God done through the life of His son Jesus. Judas spent hours on end, day after day, year after year, basking in the love and power of the creator of the world. Yet, he would fall from that high calling down to the very depths of Satan's horrid control. What happened to Judas' heart?

> "And supper being ended, the devil having already *put it in*to the **heart** of Judas Iscariot, Simon's son, to betray Him,...Now after the piece of of bread, Satan *entered* him. Then Jesus said to him, 'What you do, do quickly.'" JOHN 13:2, 27

Wow! Not a good day for Judas. Not a good life for Judas. How did this happen? Where did it all start? I do not believe these questions can be answered definitively; the fact that it did is enough to ponder. Obviously it did not happen all at once. Even in these closing hours there were two fatal steps. First the devil had access to his heart ("the devil put it into his *heart*"). Second Satan took control of his life ("Satan entered him"). Before Satan could take control of his soul or life, he had to have control of Judas' heart. We can learn a lot in Scripture by acknowledging what is missing or not expressed. God did not say that Satan overpowered his mind. Satan went where life exists—the heart. Gaining influence over the heart of Judas gave Satan access

A Smarter Heart

to his soul. I am not saying that our minds are not important or that they should not be guarded. I have no interest in belittling the importance of our minds. I simply want to do what Scripture reveals and place the higher importance where God does, on the heart. The following Gospel accounts make this point even clearer.

> "When anyone hears the word of the kingdom, and does not understand it, then the wicked one comes and snatches away what was sown in his **heart**. This is he who received seed by the wayside."
> MATTHEW 13:19

> "And these are the ones by the wayside where the word is sown. When they hear, Satan comes immediately and *takes* away the word that was sown in their **hearts**."
> MARK 4:15

> "Those by the wayside are the ones who hear; then the devil comes and *takes* away the word out of their **hearts**, lest they should believe and be saved." LUKE 8:12

As you may well remember, the setting for these verses is the *Parable of the Sower* told by Christ. Each gospel is slightly different while maintaining the entire truth expressed by Jesus. One thing is constant in each rendering. The word is sown in the heart. The heart is the place where the gospel message is meant to take root. Satan knows this quite well. In the gospel of Matthew he "snatches" it away before it can take root. In Mark, Satan "immediately" takes it away. And in Luke the devil takes it away "lest they believe". After hearing the word, "believing" takes place in the heart. Satan wants to get to us before the Word of God has taken root in our heart. He wants access to our hearts before we come to the place of believing grace. The process of salvation begins and ends in the heart. This will be dealt with in greater detail later. Each of these accounts describes the evil one differently. Matthew calls him "the wicked one". Mark calls him Satan, and Luke uses the title, "the devil". Putting all three of these accounts together makes it clear that we are dealing with God's enemy—the serpent. We do not want this snake in the garden of our heart. We must not allow him the slightest access.

> "And Peter said, 'Ananias, why has Satan *filled* your **heart** to lie to the Holy Spirit and keep back part of the price of the land for yourself? You have not lied to men but to God... Why have you conceived this thing in your **heart**? You have not lied to men but to God. Then Ananias, hearing these words, fell down and breathed his last..." ACTS 5:3-5

This is a very telling passage of Scripture. Satan was able to gain access to the heart of a believer in the first century Church. Ananias is a specific person with a specific name. This is not a story of what could potentially happen to the masses. This is an account of what did take place in the life of an individual person and the horrific consequences of his actions. The punishment was harsh and served as a solid warning to every believer from that day to the present.

His life was cut short, along with the life of his wife who was caught in the same lie. Peter asked Ananias why Satan had filled his heart. Satan is the author of lies, and with a lie he filled Ananias' heart. The inference in the question is that Ananias had a choice to resist Satan's evil scheme, but he chose to yield rather than resist. This is made clear in Peter's question, "Why have you conceived this thing in your heart?" The seed of this fatal action was planted by Ananias. He gave Satan the opportunity to work in his heart by first "conceiving" the idea himself. The battle with Satan takes place in your heart, and it is a battle that you can win. We are assured in I John 4:4 that, "He (Christ) who is in you is greater than he who is in the world (Satan)". Satan cannot fill our heart with evil if we do not first allow him access to our heart. We can keep the door of our heart closed to Satan by keeping it constantly open to God.

> "You have neither part nor portion in this matter, for your **heart** is not right in the sight of God. Repent therefore of this your wickedness, and pray God if perhaps the *thought* of your **heart** may be forgiven you." Acts 8:21-22

The book of Acts is a wonderful history of the early Church. It is history that we can learn from, not just collectively, but individually. There are many "heart lessons" in the book of Acts, and this one has many facets. The account gives us a look inside the heart of a man named Simon. At this time the Church was going through great persecution by the hand of Saul and other Jewish leaders. This created even greater motivation to preach the gospel by the Apostles. Philip was

An Unreliable Heart

doing just this thing, preaching Christ to the inhabitants of Samaria. Great revival took place with miracles in abundance. Unclean spirits were cast out, many people were healed, and the paralyzed walked. There was great joy throughout the entire city. Multitudes became converted to Christ.

A man named Simon who formerly practiced witchcraft and was seen as a "great power of God" by the Samaritans, soon heeded the message preached by Philip. He became a believer and in turn became extremely interested in the power of God that he witnessed at the hand of Philip. Then Peter and John arrived and laid hands on the new believers, baptizing them in the Holy Spirit. Simon was astonished and offered the apostles money that he too might possess this power for himself. I guess you could say he was all about power. It is not all about power; it is all about the heart. Simon thought he could gain with money this gift from God of "laying on hands" to receive the Holy Spirit. Peter addresses Simon's folly by informing him that he has no part in the matter because his "heart is not right in the sight of God." He commands him to repent of his wickedness in order to receive forgiveness for the "thought of his heart". Again we are reminded that the heart is capable of thinking. And in the case of Simon his heart does it poorly. God judged his heart and found it lacking. Fortunately Simon made the first right step in experiencing healing for his heart. He asked for prayer that his bitterness and iniquity would be forgiven.

A HEART OUT OF CONTROL

How far can an evil heart take us from God? Can a heart be out of the reach of God? The business of the human heart must not be taken lightly. God makes it abundantly clear that it is of eternal importance. The stakes are very high, but God is willing and able to work in us for his glory. This requires on our part a willing heart.

> "Therefore God gave them up to uncleanness, in the *lusts* of their **hearts**, to dishonor their bodies among themselves, who exchanged the truth of God for the lie, and worshiped and served the creature rather than the Creator, who is blessed forever."
> ROMANS 1:24-25

God is a gentleman. He does not force us to do his will. Even though his will is always the best choice. If we allow our heart to become corrupt it will struggle to choose God. Many have allowed lust to rule in their hearts to the point that fleshly desires rule over spiritual and eternal gain. The cost is two-fold: the suffering experienced in the flesh, and the loss of the spiritual blessing experienced now and forever. God made our earthly bodies. That reason alone is enough to cause us to place on it high value. Yet in our day, many place little value on their bodies by engaging in any number of things that cause it harm. Do I need to list some or have they already come to mind? Addictions, diseases and abuses of all kinds await those who dishonor their earthly bodies, often resulting in an early grave. The same God who made your earthly body will make your eternal body. It is a mighty work of God both ways. Your heart will make the choice on whether or not eternity is spent in the presence of God.

> "But in accordance with your hardness and your *impenitent* **heart** you are

treasuring up for yourself wrath in the day of wrath and revelation of the righteous judgment of God." ROMANS 2:5

Yes, we need a reminder. This is the business of the heart, not the mind. The mind is involved, but the heart takes the lead. What does it mean to be "impenitent"? It simply means an unwillingness to repent. Not choosing to turn around, to flee evil, and go the other direction. This choice is made in the heart. The more we resist repentance, the harder our heart becomes. Do you remember those Scriptures on the treasures of a good or evil man? Both are treasuring up something, one good things, the other bad. It is clear here that the bad treasure can end up being a treasure case full of wrath in the Day of Judgment. These are harsh words, but they are God's righteous words preparing us for His righteous judgment. His desire is to reward each one of us. But the choice is ours - a heart choice. We must learn to make righteous choices of the heart now lest we "have a *heart* trained in covetous practices" (II Peter 2:14). The *heart* can be trained for good or evil. Ecclesiastes 9:3 teaches about men trained in evil that "...madness is in their hearts while they live, and after that they go to the dead."

In the book of Jeremiah we find "heart" used 62 times. Obviously the condition of the heart was important to this great prophet of God. The prophet Jeremiah had a long ministry admonishing the people of God to reject the false gods of Babylon and remain loyal to the one true God. This loyalty was a function of their hearts. The prophet Jeremiah uses the term "dictates" eight times when discussing the heart in a manner that suggests a heart so well trained that it commands instruction with authority. The heart can become well trained, efficiently dispensing either good or evil. The prophet Jeremiah speaks to the results of a heart trained in evil. Your heart can become a dictator of evil or good, either way, it is your heart. I like to think of it as going on "auto pilot", or "cruise control". In both cases you are still in the driver's seat. It is your heart directing you toward good or evil.

I can clearly remember a frightening experience I had as a small boy on the farm. I was placed on a large horse for my first solo ride. We trotted down the lane for about a mile when the horse decided on a course of his own. He was soon dictating the direction my life would take, holding the reins had little effect on the outcome. Fortunately he was a good horse with a good heart and at the end I was safely back home where we started. The horse did the right thing even though I would have preferred to have been in control. I really don't think I was ever in control. I believe we would all enjoy a heart that was trained in righteousness, leading us down a road of joy and contentment, not pain and destruction. How is this possible? How can we be certain that our heart will "dictate" good? Can we know without doubt that our heart will lead us to our Father's eternal home? These questions will be answered as we look at the heart that can be trusted.

Ponder this in your Heart

If we have wickedness in our heart, then Satan has access to our heart. Is there anything in your heart that would allow Satan to influence your life?

CHAPTER FIVE | A Trustworthy Heart

> "The *Heart* is deceitful above all things and desperately wicked; *who can know it?* I the Lord search the **heart**, I test the mind, even to give every man a according to his ways, according to the fruit of his doings."
> Jeremiah 17:9-10

You are probably asking why I started this chapter on a good heart with a Scripture describing a wicked heart. Simply put, we must continue to understand that God's focus is on man's heart, whatever its condition. The corrupt heart must be changed, and the mind is under God's scrutiny as well. They work together with the heart taking the lead. Man's conduct is dictated by his heart, and his actions bring forth either good or bad results; a harvest of good or bad "fruit". The root of this fruit producing plant is the heart. If the plant is in need of healing, it must begin with the root.

Many folks are familiar with a plant killing product called Roundup. I have used it many times on my property to kill weeds, grass, and other unwanted plants. It is extremely effective because it goes deep into the roots to initiate its destructive work. It normally takes a few days before you can begin to see its effect. The plant begins to discolor close to the ground, long before the leaves begin to die. The plant is dying from the inside out. Satan purposes to get to our heart, to destroy man from the inside out. God's design is to save man, by first reaching his heart.

Allow me to stop and make the point that the central theme of this chapter is the relationship between a trustworthy heart and salvation. The topic of faith becomes a big factor as well. But before we get into this discussion I would like to point out that salvation is not essential in enjoying many benefits of a healthy heart. In the book of Acts the story of Cornelius comes to mind. He is described as "a devout man and one who feared God with all his household, who gave alms generously to the people, and prayed to God always." (Acts 10:2) Here was a man of great generosity, who exemplified tremendous respect toward God, and was well disciplined in the practice of prayer. Sounds like a good heart to me. In fact his heart was so healthy that it positively influenced his entire household. He was a very spiritual man who found himself clearly seeing a vision of an angel from God informing him that his prayers and alms were favorable to God. The angel then instructed Cornelius to send men to the city of Joppa to speak with the Apostle Peter and receive instruction from him concerning the next step in his life. Before the men arrived God prepared Peter with a vision that was repeated three times. Long story short—Peter returned with the men to Cornelius' home and preached the gospel to the entire household. Cornelius, along with family and friends, was gloriously saved. This was the first time that Gentiles had received the Word of God unto salvation. I love this story, probably because like most of you, I too am a Gentile. God chose Cornelius because of his fruitful heart, a heart he could trust, but still not a whole heart. He had a heart that could be trusted; but went on to receive from God a heart that could be fully trusted.

A Clean Heart

> "Create in me a clean **heart**, O God. And renew a steadfast spirit within me.
> Psalms 51:10

This is a familiar verse to many. This Psalm was written by King David when Nathan the prophet confronted David after he had committed adultery with Bathsheba. David knew the root of the sin was in his heart. He went beyond asking forgiveness. It is interesting that the Scripture uses the term "create". He not only asked God to heal his heart, but to give him a new, clean heart. This is consistent with other Scriptures. One example occurred after the anointing of Saul as King when God gave him a "new heart". The prophet Ezekiel understood this well when he said; "Cast away from you all the transgressions which you have committed, and get yourselves a new *heart* and a new spirit. For why should you die, O house of Israel" (Ezekiel 18:31). There have been times in my life when I followed the example of David and cried out to God to "create in me a clean heart". I understand more clearly now the potential of that prayer, how profound and powerful it was! The Holy Spirit in me birthed the prayer, the magnitude of which I only slightly understood.

> "Now a certain woman named Lydia heard us (Paul, Silas). She was a seller of purple from the city of Thyatira who worshipped God. The Lord *opened* her **heart** to heed the things spoken by Paul." Acts 16:14

It is all about God. Salvation is made possible by God, begins with God, is completed by God, and is sustained by God. And it takes place in the human heart. The Holy Spirit led Paul and Silas to Philippi to preach the gospel. On the Sabbath, Paul and Silas spoke to Lydia and other women who were praying by the riverside. The setting was ideal for hearing the gospel; but before the message could take seed, it was necessary for God to open Lydia's heart. For the saving of the soul the message of salvation must take root in the heart. Like Cornelius, she had a heart ready to receive the Word of God.

A Believing Heart

> "But the righteousness of faith speaks in this way. Do not say in your **heart**, 'Who will ascend into heaven?' (that is, to bring Christ down from above) or, 'Who will de- descend into the abyss?' (that is, to bring Christ up from the dead). But what does it say? 'The *word* is near you, in your mouth and *in* your **heart** (that is the word of faith which we preach); that if you *confess* with your mouth the Lord Jesus and *believe* in your **heart** that God has raised Him from the dead, you will be saved. For with the **heart** one *believes* unto righteousness, and with the mouth *confession* is made unto salvation."
> Romans 10:6-10

This portion of Scripture is paramount in comprehending everything that has been discussed up to this point and everything which follows. The "heart" is mentioned four times in these five critical verses, critical from the perspective that they clearly declare the truth of eternal salvation. Contained here are seven key terms in understanding the elements of salvation. Beginning with "salvation" itself, they are: "righteousness", "faith", "the word", "confession", "believe", and the "heart". In most systematic theology books you will find little emphasis placed on the "heart"; yet these verses do place a great deal of attention there. Of course none of the elements stand alone. They all work together to form the substance of salvation.

When I attempt to make pumpkin bread every item in the recipe is essential in obtaining the desired results. Even though each ingredient has very desirable qualities in and of themselves, it is required that they be mixed together to accomplish the desired results. Each item needs to be understood and fully used. There is no doubt that the recipe would be a total failure if I left out the pumpkin. The item most often overlooked in the discussion of salvation is the human heart. When the heart is left out in the process of salvation the recipe is incomplete.

Let's take a close look at this recipe for salvation found in the tenth chapter of Romans. The sixth verse states. "But the righteousness of faith speaks in this way". This verse begs the question, what is the right kind of faith? These words speak; they have life because they hold spiritual truth. What does "righteousness" mean? Because of our sin we are separated from God. The only way this relationship can be made "right" is for us to be made "just" before God. This is made possible by the shed blood of Christ on the cross. When you cause a break in your relationship with a friend it needs to be mended, to be made "right". You say to yourself, I need to get right with them. It takes "faith" to get right with God, the right kind of faith, a faith spoken from the "heart". Noah Webster's definition of "righteousness" found in his 1828 Dictionary is very helpful in understanding "righteousness". Remember he was not only a very intelligent man but also a very devout Christian and Theologian.

Mr. Webster says that "righteousness is purity of heart and rectitude (rightness) of life; conformity of *heart* and life to the divine law. Righteousness, as used in Scripture and theology…is comprehending holy principles and affections of heart, and conformity of life to the divine law… in short, it is true religion." By his definition of "righteousness" we can conclude that Webster was quite aware of the place of the heart in salvation. Becoming right with God is a function of our heart. It is a "word of faith" spoken from the heart; that makes the "confession" that Jesus is Lord, and that God raised Him from the grave. This "word" that we speak is in our "heart". Our heart declares the truth of salvation, not our mind. Our mind does not contain these spiritual truths, the heart does. The mind is not absent; the heart simply takes the lead. This eternal "belief" takes place in the "heart", and when confessed by the heart it results in eternal life. The "heart" does the believing leading the mouth to make to make the "confession" of "faith".

I am very grateful to the Bible teachers of my young adult life who made it clear to me that salvation constituted not just a change of mind, but rather a changed heart and a new life. Christianity, as one said, "is not just a new way of thinking but a new way of living". Christianity is a changed life, not a new philosophy of living. I believe this is brought home as we grow in our understanding of the heart and allow it to take its proper role of leadership in our life. It is our heart that God uses to lead us to salvation. God changes our heart. He gives us a new heart, and therein a new life. This new life happens because we make the confession of faith in Jesus Christ with our mouth. And "out of the abundance of the *heart* the mouth speaks" (Matthew 12:34). A heart filled with the treasure of God's saving grace.

> "Then He said to them, 'O foolish ones and slow of **heart** to *believe* in all that the prophets have spoken! Ought not the Christ to have suffered these things and to enter into His glory?...Then their eyes were opened and they knew Him; and He vanished from their sight. And they said to one another, 'did not our **heart** burn within us while He talked with us on the road, and while He opened the Scripture to us....Now as they said these things, Jesus, Himself stood in the midst of them, and said to them, 'Peace to you.' But they were terrified and frightened, and supposed they had seen a spirit. And He said to them, 'Why are you troubled?' And why do doubts arise in your **hearts**?'"
> LUKE 24:25-26, 31-32, 36-38

The story of Christ on the road to Emmaus and His encounter with His Disciples immediately after is very revealing. I trust you remember how Cleopas and a companion were traveling on the third day after the crucifixion to the village of Emmaus. They were extremely troubled having expected Jesus to free them of the tyrannical rule of the Romans. Now He was dead! But they were wrong. In their sorrow Jesus appeared and continued with them to the end of their journey. They did not recognize Him.

For a good portion of the seven mile journey Jesus just listened as they explained the events that had taken place in Jerusalem. They talked about the crucifixion of Christ and how they were astonished to hear that a certain women in their group had visited the tomb and found it empty. She also was comforted by angels declaring that Jesus was alive. They added that others had visited the tomb as well, and found that it was exactly as the woman reported. Then Jesus spoke. "O foolish ones, and slow of heart to believe in all that the prophets have spoken!" He admonished them for not believing the prophetic words of the Scriptures. He did not accuse them of having disbelieving thoughts but rather a sluggish heart. A heart that was slow to believe the truth of Scripture. As common as the word "slow" seems to be, it is not the case here. In the original Greek form "bradus" it is used only one other time in the New Testament. God is picking His terms carefully. The word means dull, inactive, and stupid. It is really kind of humorous. He did not accuse them of being stupid mentally, but rather having a stupid heart. A heart that was lacking, slow to comprehend and believe the truth of Jesus Christ.

In our need and confusion Christ leads us to God's word. From that point on He taught them concerning Moses and the prophets expounding from the Scriptures those things that concerned Himself. As we know from the account of Christ being tempted by Satan in the wilderness, He did not do this to exalt Himself in arrogance. In response to each of Satan's three advances Jesus turned the Devil's attention to the Word of God by saying "It is written" and then quoting the appropriate Scripture. God desires to make a lasting union between His word and our heart. That makes for a heart that is quick to believe God and willing to follow His ways completely. Our heart must believe that in the resurrection Christ was glorified and that we too may rise and walk in newness of life.

Cleopas and his companion did not recognize Jesus until the end of the journey when He ate with them in their home. After blessing the food He vanished from their sight. Then they knew it was Him and quickly remembered how their hearts burned within them as He taught them from the Scriptures. Their hearts were aware of Him all along, but they were slow to believe. Now with fresh energy, they turned around and went back to Jerusalem to share with their brethren this wonderful experience with Jesus. As they shared, Christ appeared in their midst. The group's response was instant fear. They thought they saw a spirit. Again He addressed the heart. He focused on their "doubting" hearts and comforted them by revealing His wounds, convincing them that it truly was He. We also do our share of doubting; but if we will allow Christ to lead our hearts through the Scriptures we too will experience what those early followers felt as they walked with Christ.

A WISE HEART

Certainly a wise heart is a heart that can be trusted. Most certainly a heart wise enough to accept Christ as the living God and then continue on in relationship with Him for all eternity. In that scenario we can expect nothing less than growing in the wisdom of God. I am reminded again of King Solomon, the wisest man who ever lived. When Solomon cried out for wisdom he was setting an example for all of us who followed.

A Smarter Heart

> "Therefore give your servant an *understanding* **heart** to judge your people that I may discern between good and evil... Behold I have done according to your words; see, I have given you a wise and *understanding* **heart** so that there has not been anyone like you before you, or shall any like you arise after you."
>
> I Kings 3:9, 12

I could easily see how Solomon may have been overwhelmed with the thought of his new found position as King. He was following in the footsteps of his father David who reigned in a phenomenal manner. As he envisioned the task ahead he did not seek God for greater mental intellect. As many of us have thought in the past, he did not desire great wisdom of mind. Solomon asked God for an "understanding heart". I was completely taken by surprise when God first showed me this fact in Scripture. For my entire life I thought Solomon asked God for mental wisdom. Solomon believed that the ability to discern between evil and good and thus judge his people correctly required a change in his heart. Rather than ask God for a higher IQ he asked God to increase understanding in his heart.

In answer to Solomon's prayer, God not only gave him an understanding heart but added wisdom of the heart as well. God did this in great abundance, informing Solomon that he would be wiser than anyone before him and everyone after him. That would make him the wisest man who ever lived. But let us not forget that this great wisdom and understanding resided in his heart. I am glad that I do not always get what I pray for. Sometimes I pray for the wrong thing. Solomon's prayer teaches us well the importance of praying correctly. If we pray from the heart, led by the Holy Spirit, the results in our life will be profound.

> "And God gave Solomon wisdom and *exceedingly great* understanding and *largeness* of heart like the sand of the seashore. I Kings 4:20

God repeats Himself intentionally as a way of emphasizing a point of truth. In Chapter five of I Kings it is repeated that Solomon's prayer was answered, receiving an understanding heart from God. But God also adds the adjective "exceedingly great". The point is being driven home in an emphatic way. The intellectual power of Solomon's heart, not his mind, would be beyond the imagination of man's mind. And this is exactly how people reacted to him. They were amazed, laymen and leader alike. God does not stop here. He communicates even more forcefully when He adds "largeness of heart" to the description of the work being done in Solomon's soul. Capacity was being added to contain this great wisdom. But just how great would this increase be? God paints on a large canvas, when he says, "like the sand of the seashore". That is a huge increase in the size of Solomon's heart. That heart could contain a tremendous amount of wisdom, beyond our wildest imaginings. An enlarged heart is available for any of God's children who openly seek to do His will and experience His best in their lives. This is substantiated in Psalms 119 where "heart" is spoken of fifteen times with an emphasis on "largeness" in verse thirty two where it says, "I will run the course of Your commandments, for You shall enlarge my heart".

I was overwhelmed when I initially grappled with this description of the expanse of Solomon's heart. It seemed to me an exaggeration. But perhaps God was describing a heart of infinite capacity. Even in the natural our bodies have an element of infinite built into them. If we take just one cell, say a heart cell, and use increasing magnification we can go deeper and deeper, encountering additional mysteries within. I talked about this in the first chapter when discussing the brain. As scientists develop new tools for penetrating the cells or neurons of the brain, they make profound discoveries. The same would be true investigating heart cells, especially when observing neurons in the heart. Just as the universe expands out infinitely, God's human creation expands infinitely inward. I like to call this the "inner universe". Eternity is very difficult for the mind to comprehend, perhaps even frightening. But the heart is capable of embracing the infinite. Possibly Ecclesiastes 3:11 "...He has put eternity in their *hearts*..." has greater meaning than we could ever imagine.

There is much more that we can learn from Solomon's life, which we will do later as we continue our study into the miracle of His life. Solomon provides us with an amazing perspective into the workings of a successful life, success that continued only when his heart remained loyal to God.

A Pure Heart

Is a "pure" heart analogous with a "perfect" heart? When the Scripture speaks of a person who is "above approach", does this mean they are living a perfect life, absent of any sin? What does Jesus mean in the Sermon on the Mount when He says, "Be perfect as your heavenly Father is perfect"? Does this mean we are never to error in our thinking or conduct? What did the writer of Hebrews mean when he said, "...let us go onto perfection..."? Peter says it this way in his first epistle, "...be holy in all your conduct..." Psalms 101:2 declares, "...I will walk within my house with a perfect *heart*". There have been Bible scholars who were convinced that personal perfection was possible on this side of heaven. In fact I know of at least one denomination that held this belief as one of its early tenants of faith. I am not intending to explicitly answer my own questions. I am not certain that the best questions are being presented. But I am certain of this, that any person who has truly given their heart over to Christ has the potential of living a victorious life. A life that rises far above the sin that purposes to enslave us. The Christ empowered heart is the source and means to this overcoming life. Yes, we can be more than conquerors!

> "So God who knows the **heart** acknowledged them by giving them the Holy Spirit, just as He did us, and made no distinction between us and them, *purifying* their **hearts** by faith."
> ACTS 15:8, 9

The back drop to this verse was a discussion among the Apostles concerning the recent conversion of Gentiles and their potential adherence to the Law of Moses. They received a glorious salvation, were baptized in water, and were filled with the Holy Spirit. But this verse speaks of an added element in the experience that is too often over looked. Their hearts were purified. What exactly does this mean? Pollution holds the opposite meaning of pure. For many decades we have made a concerted effort to clean up our environment and keep it in that state. Keeping the streams, lakes, forests, fields, and skies clean is a relentless task, requiring the effort of every citizen. But there is a greater need to purify the human heart. The pollution of iniquity that had lodged in the hearts of these early Christians was eradicated immediately. Sin and death no longer had power over them. They were free to grow in the grace of Christ.

> "Flee also youthful lusts; but pursue righteousness, faith, love, peace with those who call on the Lord with a *pure* **heart.**" II TIMOTHY 2:22

Maintaining a pure heart takes constant diligence. Thankfully the power of the Holy Spirit in our lives makes that a reality. We must take the first step of action by fleeing lust. But that in itself is not sufficient. Then we are admonished to pursue those qualities of the Spirit-filled life which Christ Himself demonstrated in His ministry on Earth. Righteousness, faith, love, and peace seem to cover every element of a Godly life directed by a pure heart. This is a life that is in right relationship with God, living by faith in love, enjoying a continual peace that cannot be taken away

> "Now the purpose of the commandment is love from a *pure* **heart**, from a good conscience, and from sincere faith."
> I TIMOTHY 1:5

> "Let us draw near with a *true* **heart** in full assurance of faith, having our **hearts**

> sprinkled from an evil conscience and our
> bodies washed with pure water."
> HEBREWS 10:22

A clear conscience is very powerful. It has always been maintained that our conscience is embodied in our brains. Perhaps there is more to it than we think. The Bible teaches that the "conscience" of our "heart" must be washed clean from evil. For many it is quite difficult to overcome the guilt of a bad conscience. Perhaps failure continues because the tool of choice to repair the problem is the "power of the mind", rather than "love from a pure heart". A hammer is absolutely necessary when building a house, but is rarely used when repairing an automobile engine. Right thinking or the power of positive thinking will not do the trick. The evil is creating the greatest damage in the heart not in the mind. Seeking forgiveness from the heart and making amends by the power of love in the heart will bring about the desired outcome—a pure heart.

> "Draw near to God and He will draw
> will draw near to you. Cleanse your
> hands, you sinners; and *purify* your
> **hearts**, you double-minded."
> JAMES 4:8

An unclean heart will lead to unclean hands and then to evil behavior. A heart given over to evil will produce a "double-minded" man. We have heard of people with one or more additional personalities. This verse is not addressing multiple personality disorders. In fact those cases are relatively rare in the world. So what does it mean to be "double-minded"? This term is used only two times in the New Testament, both in James. The other use is found in James 1:8, "he is a double minded man unstable in all his ways". In the Old Testament when this same subject is addressed the word "double-hearted" is used. Some commentators of the Bible have pointed out that the original Greek word "dipsukos" may be better translated, "double-souled". An early and well accepted scholar, Adam Clarke (1762 -1863) took 27 years to write his commentary on the Bible. It was published in eight large volumes in 1826. This is what he had to say on the subject. A double minded man is " a man of two souls, who has one for earth and another for heaven; who wishes to secure both worlds; he will not give up earth, and he is loath to let heaven go." To my way of thinking, he is a man whose heart and mind are in a constant argument. He is unwilling to yield to the potential of a spiritual heart, believing that the power of the flesh will bring about eternal benefits. It is little wonder that he is "unstable in all his ways".

A healthy heart desires that we seek God and that we do it with all that is in us. A half-hearted man is destined to be a double-minded man. As one commentator said, "The double-minded is at fault in the heart." The path to a mature and whole mind is a pure heart, given completely to the pursuit of God and His ways.

PONDER THIS IN YOUR HEART

The surest way to obtain a whole and healthy heart is to give it to God. God who judges your heart has the desire and power to change your heart. If that is your wish, then make it known to God in prayer.

CHAPTER SIX | Live Whole Heartedly

This is where the rubber meets the road. If we want to gain traction in the Christian walk a key principle must be engaged, if not we will continue just spinning our wheels. That "key" principle means giving it our highest and strongest effort. Many Christians find themselves in a constant struggle to effectively live a victorious and successful life. Some are caught in the guilt of past sin and failure. Others cannot seem to find a meaningful place in God's work. There are those that know that they are exactly where they need to be but just don't seem to be experiencing any real success whatsoever. You may have found the previous chapter's eye opening and encouraging, providing great hope for the pilgrimage ahead. But if a light-hearted approach is taken the results will be shallow and your new goals and dreams will not take root. If an "all out" approach is your choice, then the Word of God will be abundantly lived out in your life. The results will be beyond your wildest imaginings.

Trusting God Fully From the Heart

Does God ever ask us to do something we are incapable of performing? In our own strength many things are unattainable, but with God nothing is impossible. This is difficult in the beginning for our brains to grasp; but a heart yielded to God will lead our mind and souls in believing. We can trust God completely!

> "Trust in the Lord with *all* your **heart**,
> and lean not on your own understanding
> In *all your* ways acknowledge Him,
> and He shall direct your paths."
> Proverbs 3:5-6

This is a favorite verse for many. My mother has had this verse on her wall for years. She has cherished it for decades in her heart. Not just because it sounds hopeful and encouraging, but because God has proved it true over and over again in her long and fruitful life. Perhaps this is the case for you as well, I hope so!

There are some small but significant words that require our thoughtful attention. The first of these is the word "*all*". This word covers everything; nothing is excluded. We all learned this thoroughly in our early elementary schooling. It is simple math. If Dick has three apples, and he gives three to Jane and has zero left over. He has given all, that is, he has given up one hundred percent of his apples. There is nothing left over to give. This is the level of trust required to live the Christian life. This magnitude of trust does not come from the mind, but from the heart. We must trust the Lord with one hundred percent of our heart. My experience has taught me that it is a lot easier to trust totally with the heart than with the mind. It seems that this is exactly how God designed the heart to be used. As studied earlier in this book, our biological heart is a small pump that runs on electrical power. Electric motors, unlike gas engines, are capable of running for extremely long periods of time at full speed. We are to "trust" the Lord with our entire heart, running at full power, rather than trusting upon the limitations of our own way of thinking.

"Not" is another key word in this proverb. This is a word common in most languages. In German it is "nicht", in Russian "niete", in Scottish "nocht", in Danish "niet". They all have the same meaning—"nothing". "Not" denies the existence of the subject at hand even denying its being. What we are left with is a void. In the seventh chapter of Job, he addresses God saying, "Thine eyes are open upon me and I am not" KJV. In his current situation Job felt his life was worth nothing. To emphasize the same meaning, a couple places in the Kings James Version of the Bible use the word "naught". Proverbs 20:14 reads, "It is naught (nothing), it is naught (nothing), saith the buyer: but when he has gone his way, then he boasteth". In this case the buyer is being totally dishonest; speaking the exact opposite of what was true. God always speaks the truth in perfect form. God says no to putting our confidence in our own intellect at the expense of a whole hearted trust in the Lord.

What is the result of trusting God with our entire heart and disciplining our mind to follow its lead? The fruit is a lot of right decisions. This Proverb instructs us to acknowledge God in everything, and in so doing, He will direct. But with God it is all or nothing, not part and parcel.

On a beautiful late spring day, after the last semester test of my first year of Bible College, I found myself sitting on the dorm steps contemplating whether I would return the following year. Mom had asked all four of her boys to take their first year of college at a Bible school. I wanted to attend a University and study for a high school teaching diploma and a certificate in guidance counseling. I had it all figured out. My parents had recently moved to a town not far from a good university. The tuition was considerably less, and I could live with my parents and save even more money. That was my "understanding". Only one problem, I felt a tug on my heart suggesting something different. How could I be certain I was making the right decision? Should I continue at the Bible College or transfer to the University. I opened up my Bible and God led me to some timely Scriptures. As I continued reading the Scriptures jumped off the pages and spoke to my heart. I do not remember exactly what portion of Scripture caught my attention, but most assuredly, the will of God for me became crystal clear. God, using His written word, via my heart, guided me to the right path. I was at a fork in the road, and the path I chose would make a difference for years to come.

I am reminded of a testimony Peter Iliyn shared with me many years ago. Peter at the time was the Assistant Director of the Youth With A Mission base in Salem Oregon. He currently is the North American Director of YWAM. I was greatly encouraged as He shared portions of his father's story. His father, Vanya Iliyn, in 1933 as a young boy, with his family and other Christians, left Russia on foot in search of freedom. The night they left town, they walked together down the middle of the street, singing praises to God in the midst of their enemies. This was exactly as Psalms 23 promises, "Yea. though I walk through the valley of the shadow of death, I will fear no evil; For You are with me;...You prepare a table before me in the presence of my enemies;". They traveled for thousands of miles through China and Asia. At one point in the desert they were without water, face to face with death. God demonstrated his overflowing love by leading them to abundant water under the sand. Their journey would take 23 years ending in San Francisco. Many times they found themselves at a fork in the road. They quickly learned that to remain safe from evil they desperately needed God's leading. God was always faithful, when in prayer they cried out to Him for direction. Over and over again He led them down the right path. God speaks to His children! The results were devastating when on a few occasions they chose to "lean upon their own understanding". Peter has recently made this epic story available in book form. It is a must read for anyone who really wants to grow in their walk of faith. You can order, *Out Of The Far Corners* by Peter Iliyn at www.outofthefarcorners.com.

    Early in my Christian life, books like this inspired me to seek the voice of God in my decision making, and though my story is not as profound as Vanya Iliyn's, it still illustrates the importance of trusting your heart when seeking God's direction. When I chose to continue on and graduate at the Bible College; a path was established that led to many significant experiences. That first year back I established a friendship with a student of high Christian caliber. Roger and I would share an apartment together and encourage each other in a daily mid-afternoon prayer session. In answered prayer, I became part of a Christian singing group. This had been a dream of mine for a long time. But most important of all, I met my future wife, Carolyn. That choice of listening to a God-inspired heart, led me down a path with many forks, each one requiring direction from God. And at this point on the path, I find myself sitting in front of a computer screen thinking about my wife, five children, and nine grandchildren while endeavoring to write a book. By the way, along with a graduate degree I did end up getting a college level teaching and counseling certificate, along with many opportunities to counsel, teach and preach.

A Smarter Heart

> "...If your sons (David's) take heed to their way, to walk before me in truth with *all* their **heart** and with *all* their soul...you shall not lack a man on the throne of Israel...Then Solomon sat on the throne of his father David, and his kingdom was firmly established."
> I Kings 2:4, 12

These verses speak to the transition of the kingship from David to his son Solomon. The point has been well emphasized that we must let our heart take the lead if we are going to enjoy any lasting success in our life. But that in itself is not sufficient. That little word "*all*" swings the momentum in a favorable direction. My oldest son Mark is currently putting the finishing touch on two years of sailing lessons. Although I have not sailed with him yet, I am confident that when I do, he will position the sails at the correct angle to properly catch the power of the wind, and propel us with the desired speed in the correct direction. I am sure that principle is taught in Sailing 101. But without that starting point, the sailing trip to other parts of the world will never happen. The adventure of 'other worlds' in the Christian life can only happen when we give it all of our heart. And because Solomon did exactly as he was admonished, he eventually took his father's place on the throne, where he had the intelligence to ask God for an "*understanding heart* to judge" his people. Long before David and his son Solomon, God desired His children to give it their all.

> "Oh that they had such a **heart** in them that they would fear me and always keep *all* My commandments." Deuteronomy 5:29

God knows a half hearted attempt at the Christian life is no life at all. The word "*always*" provides additional emphasis to that small but poignant word "*all*". God not only wants us to give our all; but to do so continually. Is a heart totally yielded to God capable of consistently obeying God? I believe it is. And I believe the mind cooperates in this endeavor, only when it is following the lead of the heart. We must totally engage our heart!

Loving God Fully From the Heart

"You shall love the Lord with *all your* **heart**, with *all* your soul and with *all* your strength. And these words which I command you today shall be *in* your **heart**." Deuteronomy 6:6,7

"Jesus said to him, 'You shall love the Lord your God with *all* your **heart**, with *all* your soul, and with *all* your mind'." Matthew 12:37

"...with *all* your **heart**...soul...mind...strength." Mark 12:30

"...with *all* your **heart**...soul...strength...mind." Luke 10:27

After the children of Israel had been traveling in the desert for three months, having escaped the bondage of Egypt; God by the hands of Moses, at Mount Sinai, gave them His statutes, laws, and commandments. In these verses God is not suggesting, asking, or even requesting; He is requiring total and complete allegiance. What is wrong with that?

God has the necessary love to empower each of us with the desire and ability to serve Him with a whole heart. This is called the "grace" of God. The apostle Paul said; "By the grace of God, I am what I am, and His grace toward me was not in vain; but I labored more abundantly than they all, yet not I, but the grace of God which was with me" (I Corinthians 15:10). Of course it is "unmerited favor", and more. It is the power to walk in God's favor. The heart contains this power. The power of God is in our hearts.

With the command to love God totally He included a huge empowerment. God placed every commandment He had made that day in their hearts. Again let us be reminded that God did not say that He had placed them in our mind. But because of the tremendous amount of emphasis placed on our mental achievements, the mind is where we instinctively go to execute the obedient response. God has made it a heart empowerment, not a mental conquest. We will begin to experience a full joy in loving God when we enjoy and express our love fully from the heart.

This command to love God with total love is abundant throughout the entire Bible. The instruction often includes "soul" and "mind" and "strength". No matter what is included in the list, it always leads out with "heart", and then "soul". I do not believe this is by chance. God wants our heart to take the lead; this is totally consistent with Scripture. The "soul" is the essence of our "person". It is our individuality which makes us distinct from other humans. Our soul includes our own unique personality traits, intelligence, emotions, etc. It keeps our feet planted on planet earth. It is who we are. It is our person. The person God intended you to be can only be realized by totally submitting to your heart, as it is fully yielded to God. The yielded

Live Whole Heartedly

and empowered heart releases us to love God with "all our soul". This in turn renews our "mind" to fully love God. And all this is energized by the "strength" God provides the power of God within us. As a side note; the word "mind" is missing from the Deuteronomy passage because it is often translated "heart" in the Old Testament. To use it in this verse would have been a point of repetition to the early Hebrew way of thinking.

Let me illustrate the "heart", "soul", "mind", "strength" interaction by drawing our attention to the automobile. The automobile is your "soul", and without the individual parts working together it is not going anywhere. It will just gather dust in the corner of the garage. The first priority is to get the engine or heart running again, without it the other parts are meaningless. Presently, computers or the mind are an essential part of the engine. These computers run many, varying aspects of the automobile, from braking, to shifting, to acceleration. When the intellect of the engine fails, it shuts down immediately. With the complete engine package running smoothly the power can be transferred to the transaxle, or strength. The transaxle is made up of transmission, axle, and wheels. With the wheels spinning we can go places. Of course the driver of this marvelous machine is the Holy Spirit. Unfortunately this illustration is somewhat limited, because the human soul is unlike anything else in creation. What can be compared with it?

Let's spend some more time discussing these key words. The "heart" is the seat or source of physical and spiritual life. The Hebrew word for heart in the Old Testament is "lehv". This term is used when discussing nearly all aspects of the heart. It is even used when talking about the physical heart. In II Samuel 18:14, the death of Absalom the son of

King David is described. "Then Joab said, 'I cannot linger with you. And he took three spears in his hand and thrust them through Absalom's heart, while he was still alive in the midst of the terebith tree." To me this is eye opening. I believe this truth helps us to use a physical entity, our physical beating heart; to focus on, and engage our spiritual heart. When I see the need to be certain my heart is fully engaged in my present circumstance, I will place my hand firmly on my chest, my bosom, the resting place of my heart, and thump it repeatedly. This is a physical reminder to me that I need to understand and communicate with my spiritual heart. It is my way of increasing my spiritual awareness and sensitivity. At this point the Lord often reminds me of Scripture verses that I have "hid in my heart". Another occasion for the use of "lehv" when mentioning the physical heart is found in II Kings 9:24. "Now Jehu drew his bow with full strength and shot Jehoram between his arms; and the arrow came out of his heart, and he sank down in his chariot." It is also used in Psalms 37:15. "Their sword shall enter their own *heart*"; and again in Psalms 45:5. "Your arrows are sharp in the heart of the King's enemies".

It is nearly impossible to cleanly separate the physical, emotional, intellectual, and spiritual heart. There is far more spirituality in our physical lives than we ever thought possible. I spent the greater portion of my growing up days, living in small logging towns in Oregon. I remember walking into a lumber mill for the first time, to observe the production of plywood. After curing in ponds, large fir tree trunks were positioned on gigantic lathes where thin strips of veneer were peeled off. Each veneer sheet was coated with glue then placed on top of another sheet. This was repeated until the desired thickness was obtained. This grand wood and glue laden sandwich of veneer was then placed in a large press where enormous amounts of pressure were exerted to complete the bonding process. A little trimming followed for exact measurement, and the product was ready for the lumber yard to be sold. Now try tearing it apart! Nearly impossible without the right tools; and even then pieces of wood and glue of one piece will remain on the other. The plywood was designed to stick together, just like the aspects of the human heart.

Being redundant now would be helpful in comprehending our "soul". It is life and breath, the breath of life which God breathed into nostrils of Adam and Eve. At the point that this took place man became a living soul, a living being. To understand the magnitude of these verses the word "strength" needs further explanation. "Strength" in Hebrew is "mohd", and the KJV of the Bible translates it as "might". It means to the "highest degree of effort", with the greatest force possible. In the Gospels of Mark and Luke the greek word "iskus" carries essentially the same meaning. The English equivalent means "forcefully", using the highest level of intensity and might. To sum it up, with exceeding great effort of heart, we are to love the Lord our God with all our soul. A spiritually healthy heart is capable of such a commandment.

Whole Hearted towards God's Commandments

It is a point of hypocrisy to say we are fully committed to God and then follow his commandments half-heartedly. Christ warned the Church of Laodicea saying; "So then, because you are lukewarm, and neither cold nor hot, I will vomit you out of My mouth" (Revelations 3:16). God will give us the desire and ability to walk in complete obedience; this is the grace He pours out in our lives, in our hearts. We simply need to receive in faith.

> "Blessed are those who keep His testimonies, who seek Him with the *whole* **heart**...with my *whole* **heart** I have sought You, oh let me not wander from Your commandments! Your word I have hidden in my **heart** that I might not sin against You... I will run the course of Your commandments, for You shall enlarge my **heart**...Give me understanding, and I shall keep your law, indeed I shall observe it with my *whole* **heart**...I cry out with my *whole* **heart**, hear me O Lord! I keep your statutes."
> PSALMS 119:2, 10, 11, 32, 34, 145

These verses are simply a sampling of the numerous times the Psalmist refers to following God's instruction with a whole heart. When God repeats Himself, we need to listen more closely than usual. When He is extremely repetitive, the point is clear, and we are compelled to obey enthusiastically. In order to get the result promised by God, we need to abandon ourselves fully to Him from the heart. What can we learn from these verses that will instruct us on how we can experience the potential of a heart fully committed to God? First, we are to seek God with a "whole *heart*". We are not to wait passively in doing His will, but to pursue the Lord directly and not "*wander*" from His commandments. This is further emphasized in Jeremiah 29:13. "And you will seek Me and find Me, when you search for me with *all your heart*". Furthermore, we are to "run the course"; and God equips us to do so by "enlarging" our heart. God increases our capacity to do His will at all ages of our life. Joshua was advanced in years when he was instructed to "be very courageous to keep and to do all that is written in Book of the Law of Moses, lest you *turn aside from it to the right hand or to the left*" (Joshua 23:5). Many times in the Word of God this phrase is used to admonish us to stay the course and not wander off the path of righteousness. To keep things practical, let's be reminded that the mind is prone to wander, but the heart will keep us anchored.

Life flows abundantly from our heart because the Word of God is "*hidden*" in our heart. And as we will cover in detail later, Christ is the Word, and the Word is God. "In the beginning was the Word, And the Word was with God, and the Word was God" (John 1:1). God's life dwells in our heart! Pursuing God's will for our life is not necessarily easy. Often great exertion of the soul is required. That is why a total response of our heart is necessary. To gain the victory and obtain the fruit of answered prayer, we may have to "*cry out*" to God from the midst of our being, from the center of our soul. This is not mental gymnastics this is the languishing of the heart. And it gets results! The words "crying out" to God are abundant in the Bible. Dr. Bill Gothard has written a very compelling book on the subject. You can find it by contacting The Institute in Basic Life Principles. Learning the importance and blessing of crying out to God is an important element in realizing a mature heart.

"Then Philip said, 'If you believe with *all* your heart...'" Acts 8:37

This was the answer the early evangelist Philip gave to the Ethiopian Eunuch who asked him if there was any hindrance in being baptized, thus witnessing Christ as his savior. Obeying God with a whole heart begins by accepting Him as your Lord with a whole heart. From that first step on, a whole hearted effort in obeying Christ will result in consistent growth and maturity in your Christian walk. This will always be true no matter how difficult that road may become. Philip, along with other early church leaders, led by example, even in the midst of their own personal struggles. In the sixth chapter of II Corinthians, Paul shared with the believers the struggles he and other disciples were facing while ministering the gospel of Christ. But in that struggle he declared, "O Corinthians! We have spoken openly to you, our heart is wide open" (v. 11). They served God and others with a whole heart. This example of leadership from the heart is seen throughout the entire Bible.

> "I (Joshua) was forty years old when Moses the servant of the Lord sent me from Kadesh Barnea to spy out the land, and I brought back word to to him as it was in my **heart**. Nevertheless my brethren who went up with me made the **heart** of the people melt, but I *wholly* followed the Lord my God." JOSHUA 14:7-8

These words were spoken to Joshua by Caleb. Years earlier twelve warriors spied out the land that God had promised the children of Israel. Only two spies, Joshua and Caleb, brought back a favorable report. The majority in this case were wrong. Unfortunately their negative attitude demoralized the nation. They had something much more serious than a bad attitude, they had a seriously damaged

Live Whole Heartedly

heart; a heart void and empty of any courage and resolve. They were in total terror! Because Caleb's report came from a healthy heart he was able to *wholly* follow the Lord. The word *"wholly"* means to be completely filled up. There was not one ounce of Caleb's soul that was not totally committed going in and out of the Promised Land. Moses had promised him his inheritance because he had "*wholly* followed the Lord" (v. 9) and Joshua immediately blessed Caleb with the inheritance, "because he *wholly* followed the Lord God of Israel" (v. 14). Caleb was forty years old when He went in to spy out the land. Now at age eighty five he said of himself; "I am as strong this day as on the day that Moses sent me; just as my strength was then, so now is my strength for war, both for going out and for coming in" (v. 11). Joshua had a strong spiritual heart that contributed to a strong physical heart; leading to superior overall strength. That is the kind of leader we should all desire to emulate. I know people today that have the same level of strength and endurance that they enjoyed decades earlier. I contribute it to their spiritual heart health. We may not see ourselves in a leadership role, but we are all leaders in one capacity or another. Most likely, all of us have had someone looking to us for guidance and encouragement. Allow your heart to provide the hope and wisdom that those around you desperately desire.

Perhaps you do not recognize that such people exist in your life. Many years ago I had the privilege of sitting under the teaching of Juan Carlos Ortiz, a pastor from South America. He had written many books on "discipleship", sharing great insight on personal evangelism. He pointed out that we are all "priests of our own parish". The members of the parish, in order, are: our immediate family, extended family, friends, neighbors, and those we work with. Count them; you may have hundreds of people, to whom you can consistently provide direction, wisdom, and encouragement. I assure you that a heart *wholly* committed to God is capable and worthy of such a ministry.

WHOLE HEARTED KINGS

The list of kings in the Old Testament is quite long. Many were bad, and some were good. What made the good kings pleasing to God? Let's take a look at a few of these kings who found favor with God.

> "Now before him (Josiah) there was no king like him, who turned to the Lord with all his **heart,** with *all* his soul, and with all his might, according to all the Law of Moses; nor after him did any arise like him." II KINGS 23:25

> "Then they (Asa and Azzariah) entered into a covenant to seek the Lord God of their fathers with *all* their **heart** and with all their soul." II CHRONICLES 15:12

> "...he is the son of Jehoshaphat, who sought the Lord with *all* his **heart**..." II CHRONICLES 22:9

> "And in every work that he (Hezekiah) began in the service of the house of God, in the law and in the commandment, to seek his God, he did it with all his **heart.** So he prospered. II CHRONICLES 31:21

"Then the king (Josiah) stood in his place and made a covenant before the Lord, to follow the Lord, and to keep His commandments and His testimonies and His statutes with *all* his **heart** and *all* his soul..."
II CHRONICLES 34:31

I strongly encourage you to study each of these kings more closely; it will be food for your soul. Each of them led out with a totally committed heart, which was followed by an energized soul. These verses begin and end with King Josiah. He received the highest praise, being honored as the greatest of all. He began that journey to greatness by making a promise to God that he would obey Him with all his *heart* and soul. Just prior to this vow Josiah had read openly and out loud to all the inhabitants of Jerusalem, "all the words from the book of the covenant". The Holy Scriptures had been ignored and lost for many years prior to his rein. When they were discovered and brought to his attention he promptly made them the focal point of Israel. Asa also led out by taking an oath, before God, to seek the Lord. All of Judah followed his example and enjoyed "rest all around". The twentieth chapter of II Chronicles tells a wonderful story of King Hezekiah leading Judah into battle against several kings and their warriors. This chapter gives wonderful instruction on winning battles. Hezekiah led the nation in prayer and fasting, acknowledging that their only hope was in God. Through the prophet Jehaziel God declared: "...Do not be afraid nor dismayed because of this great multitude, for the battle is not yours, but God's...You will not need to fight in this battle...Now when they began to sing and praise, the Lord set ambushes... and they (the enemy) were defeated" (II Chronicles 20:15,17,22). That is a great example of Godly leadership. Nevertheless, after experiencing God's deliverance, the people of Judah, did not fully follow Hezekiah. "The high places were not taken away, for as yet the people had not directed their *hearts* to the God of their fathers". (v. 33)

It always comes back to a submitted heart, and when it doesn't there is a price to pay. King Zedekiah did evil in the sight of God; "…he stiffened his neck and hardened his *heart* against turning to the Lord God of Israel" (II Chronicles 36:13). Even after many warnings from their compassionate God, Zedekiah and his priests continued in their evil, hard-hearted ways. He was the king in power when Jerusalem was taken into captivity by the king of Babylon. Let us all purpose to follow the example of the good kings, who followed a compassionate hearted God with "all their *heart* and soul".

PONDER THIS IN YOUR HEART

God requires that we serve Him completely with all our heart. Evaluate how well you have done in achieving this mandate. Do you believe it is possible to obtain this level of commitment to God?

CHAPTER SEVEN | The Heart of God

"Yes I will rejoice over them to do them good and I will assuredly plant them in this land, with all My heart and with all My soul." JEREMIAH 32:41

Where does this "whole" hearted emphasis come from? What is the source of heart greatness? The answer is clear—God! God not only created us, but He created us in His *"likeness"*, in His own similitude. "...In the day that God created man, He made him in the likeness of God...And Adam...begot a son in his own likeness, after his image, and named him Seth" (Genesis 5:1,3). Adam was patterned after God. He was similar to God in nature and qualities. And Adam's child was also made in his own image. Seth got his DNA from Adam, and Adam received his DNA from God. And essentially we received our DNA from Adam. Perhaps I am being simplistic when I say: we have a heart because God has a heart. It all starts with God. We have studied the importance of loving God with *"all"* our heart; and here in the opening verse, God sets an example of doing just that thing. Jeremiah clearly states that God has a heart, and God has a soul; and He holds nothing back, He gives it His *"all"*. We should do no less. By His power we can do no less. It is clear in Scripture that King David was a man "after God's own heart". He wanted a heart-to-heart relationship with God. I believe he wanted a heart like God's. Let's follow David's example and purpose to discover the nature of God's heart, and possess it as our own. I believe if we want the "mind of Christ", we must begin with the "heart of God".

> "...I have consecrated this house which you have built to put My name there forever, and My eyes and my **heart** will be there perpetually." I KINGS 9:3

David dearly wanted to build a house for the Lord; but the honor was passed to his son Solomon. "But the Lord said to my father David, 'Where as it was in your *heart* to build a temple for My name, you did well that it was in your *heart*;' (I Kings 8:18)". After many years of arduous and gifted labor by a multitude of builders it was dedicated by Solomon. He honored God in prayer and blessed all the nation of Israel. God responded by saying His presence would be in the temple indefinitely. I find it interesting that God defines His presence by using the terms "eyes" and "heart". Was God saying this is a place you can come and worship, experiencing my watchful gaze and encouraged by the warmth of my heart? I believe that He was, and a whole lot more. We can get no closer to God than resting next to His heart with His eyes upon us. That truly would be "resting in the Lord".

> "God is wise in **heart,** and mighty in strength. Who has hardened himself against Him and prospered? JOB 9:4

> "The counsel of the Lord stands forever. The *plans* of His **heart** to all generations." PSALMS 33:11

These two verses point out a couple of qualities that we share with God. It was an eye opener when I first became acquainted with the idea of human hearts containing and functioning in "wisdom". I was just as startled when I learned that God has a wise heart as well. Why didn't the Scriptures use the word "mind"? If we believe the Bible when it declares that we are made in the "likeness" and "image" of God, then it is only natural that our *"wisdom of heart"* originates from a God who is "wise in heart". This is exactly what king Solomon requested of God. He asked for a wise and understanding heart. Job points out that if we harden ourselves against God, prosperity will escape our grasp. This reminds me of the many times that "hard heart" appears in Scripture. We don't harden our minds against God, but rather our hearts. The battle is fought and won in the heart. The victory results in our heart beating in cadence with the heart of God. That is prosperity in itself. But like Solomon, God may add wealth also, hopefully used to advance His kingdom here on earth.

As the Bible teaches, God has plans for us, individually and collectively. I wonder what the Lord is planning. One thing is certain; those plans are formed in His heart. He has a heart for each of his children. It is fascinating that in the field of counseling, patients experience the strongest improvement when the therapist functions with a high level of warmth, caring, and empathy. As humans we respond much less favorably to technique than we do to a big heart. God has a BIG heart. I believe we are misled when we try to comprehend the Lord's plan and grasp His counsel with our own understanding rather than engaging our heart of wisdom. This is how God intended us to commune with Him, heart to heart.

GOD'S INFLUENCE ON THE HEART

It is in God's heart to work providentially in our heart. His working is always for His glory and our highest good.

A Smarter Heart

The human heart is the focus of God's attention. He is observing our inner most being, with the desire to conform our soul to His own. As Scripture teaches, we are "...clay in the potter's hand..." (Jeremiah 6). But He is not focusing on the exterior of the pot, but rather on the center - the heart.

> "But the Lord said to Samuel, 'Do not look at his appearance or at his physical stature because I have refused him. For the Lord does not see as man sees, for man *looks* at the outward appearance, but the Lord *looks* at the **heart**."
> I Samuel 16:7

Prior to this, Saul had made an unlawful sacrifice. He had flagrantly disobeyed the Lord. Samuel said to him; "You have done foolishly, you have not kept the commandment of the Lord your God...But now your kingdom shall not continue...

The Lord has sought for Himself a man after His own *heart*" (I Samuel 13:13,14). That "man" was young David. By outward appearance it did not seem possible that he was ready for such an undertaking. His older brothers, it would have appeared, were mature and ready for the task. But no, God refused each of David's brothers; their hearts were not ready. God studied David's heart and found him mature.

It is not an easy thing to ignore the physical appearance of other people with the intent of seeing them as they really are, but the heart is capable of such a challenge. Shari, my youngest child, on her recent return from mission work in Ecuador, shared a fascinating story of a single mother in Argentina. After her husband left her and her two children, Christina lived a destitute existence on the streets and in slum dwellings. To rub salt in the wound, on occasions her former husband would show off his new "trophy" wife in her presence. Well God had His own plans for Christina. One day he led her and the children to the park where they came in contact with a group of people. As it happened, this group from a local church was providing a Christ centered program for children. Christina and her children became regular visitors to the park meeting and soon after attended the church. The church reached out to her and assisted her with her physical, emotional, and spiritual needs. She and her children were gloriously saved and in time were able to live in their own apartment.

Christina being extremely grateful to the Lord for her new life was compelled to share Christ with those living horrific lives as hers once was. She led many people to Christ, and soon began providing church services in her home. This home church ministry grew and prospered as she continued to minister to drug dealers, drunkards, prostitutes, and all types of destitute people in the squalor of the city. One glorious day she was presented with a wonderful opportunity to receive medical attention at a hospital in Cuba that specialized in her physical infirmity. You see, she was blind! She could not look at the outward appearance of others; but she could trust the heart of God to lead her heart to those prepared for the gospel message. She was not distracted by their physical stature and was able to minister to their soul.

Christina made it clear to any who would listen that the higher purpose of her trip to Cuba was to share Christ with Fidel Castro. When she arrived in Cuba she went to the Palace to visit him. The guards and other staff would not allow her request even after several daily attempts. While in the hospital, receiving daily procedures, Fidel Castro's nephew was admitted. On one of his visits that Castro made to see his nephew Christina caught his attention and was able to share the good news of Christ. She was fearless, because she lived whole-heartedly for God.

The eye treatments were not successful but she continues to serve God today; experiencing many miraculous provisions to fund her work. A wonderful demonstration of God's faithfulness toward His daughter Christina is clearly seen in the death of her former husband. No, I should have worded it "her husband" because he never finalized the divorce. As Christina was growing in spiritual prosperity, her husband was gaining in temporal wealth. He had moved to Spain and become extremely wealthy; owning many properties, businesses, and bank accounts. She received his wealth as an inheritance. Of course her church ministry experienced tremendous growth by receiving God's promise, that "...all the churches shall know that I am He which searcheth the reins and *hearts*. And I will give unto every one of you according to your works" (Revelation 2:23 KJV). There is a lesson here for any who care to receive. Learn to turn a blind eye to the world and an open heart to all God's children.

> "But as we have been approved by God to be entrusted with the gospel, even so we speak, not as pleasing men, but God who *tests* our hearts." I THESSALONIANS 2:4

God has entrusted Christians with the privilege and responsibility of sharing the good news of the gospel. God trusts us to explain the way of salvation with non-believers. But this trust is not blind; it is preceded by a test—a test of heart. God did not say He tests our mind, our strength, our will, our intellect, and our soul. But He tests our heart, our heart is on trial. The heart is at the center of our very being, our soul. If our heart is up to the task our mind and soul and strength will fall in line. "Tests" in the Greek is "dohimazo", which means to discern, examine, or scrutinize with the intent to determine genuineness or authenticity. This type of testing can best be illustrated by the work of a blacksmith. My Dad was a blacksmith and welder. He began working in his father's shop at age five. As a boy, I can still remember strolling into Dad's shop, smelling the aroma of hot steel and feeling the heat of the bright colorful flying sparks. On many an occasion I observed him testing steel. He would heat the metal red hot in a forge and then pound on it with a heavy hammer, followed by a dunk in cool water. Sometimes the metal had to be dramatically reshaped and other times just slightly, but in all cases the steel had to withstand the heat. If it was too soft or brittle it would not hold up to the task for which it was being prepared. This is the kind of testing God's children go through to determine if they are ready for the next step in their usefulness for God. God is testing the genuineness of our faith, "... being much more precious than gold that perishes, though it is tested by fire..." (I Peter 1:7). Our heart is being tested as faith does its work in the heart; "But the righteousness of *faith* speaks in this way. "Do not say in your heart, 'Who will ascend into heaven?'...But what does it say? 'The word is near you, in your mouth and in your *heart*' (that is, the word of *faith* which we preach)" (Romans 10:6, 8). Acts 15:9 teaches us that God uses faith to purify our hearts. I hope this testing of our heart finds us; "tried and true", not "tried and found wanting".

> "If you faint in the day of adversity, your strength is small...If you say, 'surely we did not know this', does not He who *weighs* the **hearts** consider it? He who keeps your soul, does He not know it?" PROVERBS 24:10, 12

The word "weighs" in Hebrew is "tahchan"; and is used only three times in the Old Testament, each time in the book of Proverbs, two of which refer to the heart. It is similar to the word "tests", also meaning to prove, try, and examine; but takes it a step further. "Weighs" means to make something even and level in order to gain and maintain balance and equilibrium. God is not just judging our heart; He is conditioning it to a high level of poise and excellence. Balance is a key in athletic greatness. In order to succeed in athletics, consistency of calmness and balance must be obtained. But to really excel one must take it a step further and acquire poise. Many pro basketball players have received instruction from ballet teachers. In doing this they gained greater conditioning and substantial improvement in balance, becoming more poised on the court. Fencing is a sport that has caught my attention, although I have never given it a try. It is a discipline that demonstrates and demands poise. When the same poise in sword play is extended to the battle field it results in either life or death. Many years, if not a lifetime, of disciplined practice is required to learn the intricacies of fencing. If we choose to cooperate, God will give us a heart of balance and poise. It is a process that continues throughout our entire lives giving us victory in adversity and spiritual battles. In "weighing" our hearts, God is guarding our "souls". A whole heart is key to a mature soul.

> "You are those who justify yourselves before men, but God *knows* your **hearts**. For what is highly esteemed among men is a abomination in the sight of God." Luke 16:15

It is not uncommon to judge among ourselves with our own measuring stick. This is when the standard for right and wrong is decided by popular opinion, not a standard beyond and above ourselves, of course that standard is God. This assumes something is correct if the majority agrees it is valid. That would be like shooting at a moving target, a world without absolutes. But God's way is higher, perfect, and unfailing and it places the emphasis on man's heart, which He understands perfectly. When Scripture says God "knows" our heart it means His perception and understanding is natural and reinforced by personal observation of our conduct. Our behavior can only be justified when it falls in line with God's will. God goes beyond our behavior to its root, the condition of the heart. It seems to us that the heart is difficult to understand; but the heart is where God directs His attention, not only to reveal, but to heal. This truth becomes more profound when studying the following passages from the book of Acts.

> "And they prayed and said, 'You, O Lord, who *know* the **hearts** of all, show which of these two You have chosen." Acts 1:24

> "So God, who *knows* the **heart**, acknowledged them by giving them the Holy Spirit, just as He did to us." Acts 15:8

"Knows the heart" is one word in the Greek - "kardiognostces". These two verses are the only place where this word is used. In The New Strong's Exhaustive Concordance Of The Bible this term immediately follows the word "kardia" "heart" and is the combination of two words, "kardio" "heart" and "gnostces", meaning "knowledge". Its literal meaning is "knower of hearts". It would be as if God was given the title, Knower of Hearts. God is personally and intimately acquainted with our hearts. He prominently works in our lives in the heart. This is where it all began when we believed on Him "with the heart".

In the first passage from Acts, the apostles are in the process of choosing a replacement for Judas, who betrayed Jesus. The choice of a new Apostle was predicated on the condition of his heart. All the qualities necessary for effective mini- try are wrapped up in the heart. The totality of the human soul is summed up in the heart. God looks to the heart to determine the usefulness of His children. "Would not God search this out? For He *knows* the secrets of the *heart*" (Psalms 44:21). By searching our heart God knows who has truly accepted Him and ready to receive the Holy Spirit. This is clearly stated in the second passage chosen from Acts. The Holy Spirit is the proof and empowerment, and the essence of our new life in Christ.

> "The eyes of the Lord run to and fro through out the whole earth, to show Himself strong in the behalf of them whose **heart** is *perfect* to Him..."
> II CHRONICLES 16:9 KJV

This is a powerful and wonderful verse, filled with hope for those who desire God's power working openly in their lives. But in the past I also thought it was out of reach. When I first became acquainted with it, the Bible teacher said God was looking for that "one", and was yet to find him. Many great men of God exist today, and many have gone on before me; if they had failed to measure up, then it was unlikely that I would make the grade. As I studied the Bible, God began to show me the "truths of the heart", and this passage took on a new light. The Lord is not looking for "one" particular person; He is scouring the earth for "*them*". Many have already lived out this verse in their lives and many more will. Let me explain why this is true.

In the Hebrew the word "perfect" is "shahlehm", which means "full", "whole", "complete", and "loyal". God is not looking for a flawless person, with perfect thoughts and conduct, who does not make mistakes or even sin. The Lord is looking for someone with a particular heart; a heart that is completely and fully loyal to Him. This is attainable! The human heart, submitted completely to God, and empowered by His Holy Spirit is capable of such a feat. God has already made Himself "*strong*" in my life and by His grace will continue to do so. I look forward to the wonderful work the Lord desires to do in my heart, to be glorified through me. Is this also your desire? I trust it is.

God's Input in the Heart

> "Then I will give them one **heart** and I will *put* a new spirit within them, and *take* a stony **heart** out of their flesh, and *give* them a **heart** of flesh... I will *give* you a new **heart** and put a new spirit within you. I will *take* the **heart** of stone out of

> your flesh and *give* you a **heart** of flesh."
> EZEKIEL 11:19; 36:26

Ezekiel did all his prophesying in Babylon during the captivity of the nation of Judah. He was very flamboyant when presenting God's message. As pointed out in *The Hebrew-Greek Key Study Bible*, he would use pantomiming, cry and wail, and even ate a scroll. His book is very unique in that most of the chapters are quoted or alluded to in all but one chapter in Revelation. His prophecy has much to do with the future yet to come. In addition Ezekiel stressed the individual responsibility of one's sin in the context of Judah's national sin. This is a good reason to take his prophesy to heart. Early in their captivity God made a promise and then repeated it later. They would receive one heart and a new spirit. How is it possible that a group of people could function as if they had one heart? It seems as if there would be a lot of agreement. We certainly do not see much evidence of that "oneness" in our country today. It does not even seem possible. But nothing is impossible with God. This change of heart, God is promising to do Himself. He is going to do the *"giving"*, *"putting"*, and *"taking"*. It is a great encouragement to know that the Lord will Himself do the work that is needed in our heart and in the collective national heart as well. As God did with His chosen people, He will also do for our nation, as declared in II Chronicles 7:14. "If My people who are called by My name will humble themselves, and pray and seek My face, and turn from their wicked ways, then I will hear from heaven, and will forgive their sin and heal their land".

> "Then I arose in the night, I and a few men with me. I told no one what my God had *put into* my **heart** to do at Jerusalem...Then my God *put it into*

my **heart** to gather the nobles, the rulers, and the people, that they might be registered by genealogy."
NEHEMIAH 2:12; 7:5

Jeremiah was responsible for the rebuilding of Jerusalem as a fortified city. He did this under the authority of the leader of the Persian Empire, King Artaxerxes. God prepared him for this seemingly insurmountable task by doing a work in his heart. The Lord "*put*" specific instruction into his heart on things that needed to be accomplished. Remember God did not put this instruction into his mind, but into his heart. This same type of heart empowerment took place during the building of the tabernacle in the wilderness. "And He has put in his heart that he may teach, both he (Bezalel) and Aholiab…Them hath He *filled* with wisdom of *heart,* to work all manner of work, and of the cunning workman…" (Exodus 35:34, 35 KJV). "In the original Hebrew, "*cunning workman*" means someone with inventive talents. In addition to being talented craftsmen, they were also inventors. All the great inventions to benefit man have been done by the hand of God through those he chose. He continues today to gift men with inventive talents. The gift of inventing rests in the heart. When a work of God is at hand, an adequately equipped heart is required. Thank God that He does the equipping.

"Now may the Lord *direct* your **hearts** into the love of God and into the patience of Christ."
II THESSALONIANS 3:5

"But thanks be to God, who *puts* the same earnest care for you into the **heart** of Titus."
II CORINTHIANS 8:16

God works directly with our hearts in miraculous ways, if we will yield to Him. He guides our hearts into His love. He leads our hearts into the nature of Christ Himself. The traits that we desire, such as *patience,* can be ours as their source is in Christ. These He bestows on us by faith as we believe and practice His ways. This empowerment flows from God's heart to our heart, from the love of God filling our hearts. The Godly quality of extending care to others is not limited to those with the gift of mercy and hospitality, but for any that long to encourage and build up others. Christ desires to fill our hearts with His essence; literally with His Holy Spirit, that we may touch others with His voice and His hands. What a fabulous future He has for each one of us!

GOD DIRECTS THE HEART OF LEADERS

There are many examples of God dealing directly in the hearts of Kings, Priests, and Prophets in the Bible. There are many jewels of insight we can discover by observing the lives of God's chosen servants throughout biblical history. In Proverbs 21:1, God makes it clear that He exercises His power in the life of leaders, specifically in their heart. "The king's *heart* is in the hand of the Lord, like the rivers of waters; He *turns* it wherever He wishes." The actions taken by leaders and teachers can directly affect many people under their stewardship and care. We are reminded in James 3:1 to be cautious when undertaking the over sight of others. "My brethren, let not many of you become teachers, knowing that we shall receive a stricter judgment." Remember, teaching is executed by our actions as well as our words. It brings me great comfort to know that just as God exercised

The Heart of God

power over the hearts of kings in the Bible, He continues to do so in the hearts of world leaders today. It may not appear that way from our limited perspective, but be assured that "Jesus Christ is the same yesterday, today, and forever" Hebrews 13:8). God's hand is still working wonders today, in the hearts of leaders all over the world.

> "Then the Spirit of the Lord will come upon you, and you will prophesy with them, and be *turned* into another man...so it was, when he (Saul) had turned his back to go from Samuel, that God *gave* him another **heart**, and all these signs came to pass that day." I Samuel 10:6, 9, 10

The prophet Samuel was directed in advance by God to anoint Saul as King over Israel. He was given specific knowledge of what Saul was to do in the events that preceded him. When they met, Samuel was faithful in presenting God's instruction to Saul. Saul would be taking a big step from a farmer to king, and in the midst of this transition would find himself prophesying with the school of prophets. Not only would he prophesy, but he would be "changed into another man". God accomplished this by giving him "another heart". All the signs that the Lord had promised in the days ahead for Saul took place after his heart was changed. Ponder that for a minute. Did God give him a brand new spiritual heart, or a new physical heart? Remember, the same Hebrew term in God's inspired word describes both hearts; it is difficult to divide the two. There would be a greater strain on Saul's life in every area; physical, emotional, and spiritual. He would need a complete touch of God. Whatever the case, when God strengthens us spiritually, we are physically invigorated as well. "My son, give attention to my words...keep them in the midst of your *heart;* for they are *life* to them that find them, and *health to all their flesh"* (Proverbs 4:20, 21, 22).

> "And God gave Solomon wisdom and exceedingly great understanding and *largeness* of **heart** like the sand of the seashore. Thus Solomon's wisdom excelled the wisdom of all the men of the East and all the wisdom of Egypt." I Kings 4:29-30

God gave Solomon the capacity of heart to contain a huge amount of wisdom and intelligence. As mentioned in the beginning of this book, science has discovered that the heart can think as does the mind. It has thousands of neurons, which are the same type of cells that give the brain its ability to think, reason, and communicate. Science has made significant advances in the ability to observe and map the inner depths of neurons, proceeding further and further into the inner space of these cells. The inner workings of the heart and mind are vast, and God is capable of expanding them even further. He did it with Solomon, the wisest man on earth. He can do it for anyone He chooses.

> "Let his (Nebuchadnezzar) heart be changed from that of a man. Let him be given the **heart** of a beast." Daniel 4:16

> "But when his (Nebuchadnezzar) **heart** was lifted up, and his spirit was hardened in pride, he was deposed from his kingly throne and they took his glory from him. Then he was driven from the sons of men, his **heart** was made like the beasts, and his dwelling was with wild donkeys." Daniel 5:20, 21

The Scripture is clear that the change in Nebuchadnezzar took place specifically in his heart. The text does not emphasize other terms like "mind", "body", or "soul". The "heart", like elsewhere in Scripture, is repeated over and over again so that the reader gets the point. If the heart is changed, then the man is changed. The center of a man is his heart. This is an amazing Scripture. Nebuchadnezzar was not changed in appearance to look like a beast, although his hair and nails grew to look like eagle feathers and claws, he was given the "heart of a beast". Therefore he lived like a beast. He had become so arrogant and filled with pride that God chose to take drastic measures to gain his attention. Solomon warned that "pride goes before destruction, and a haughty spirit before a fall" (Proverbs 16:18). Pride is a sinister malady of the heart that is often undetectable by its victim. It cuts man off from God's empowering grace. "Surely He scorns the scornful, but gives grace to the humble" (Proverbs 3:34). According to *Webster's 1828 American Dictionary of the English Language*, "pride" is, "inordinate self-esteem; and unreasonable conceit of one's own superiority in talents, beauty, wealth, accomplishments, rank or elevation in office, which manifests itself in lofty airs, distance, reserve, and often in contempt of others." This is brilliantly summarized by Benjamin Franklin. "Pride that dines on vanity, sups on contempt". No wonder God finds it extremely distasteful. "The one who has a haughty look and a proud *heart*, him I will not endure" (Psalms 101:5). In Isaiah, God promises to "revive the heart" of those who are penitent toward Him. This is demonstrated in Nebuchadnezzar's life when at the end of this testing, and "understanding returned" to him, he exclaimed, "those who walk in pride He (God) is able to put down" (Daniel 4:37).

A Smarter Heart

Obviously he learned who is ultimately in charge. He may have been the ruler over the entire known world, but his heart remained in the hand of God and was vulnerable to His control. God put him in power, to begin with, and relieved him of his authority when it was fitting.

We can learn significantly from the life of Nebuchadnezzar and other great leaders in Bible history. We too find ourselves with opportunities to make a difference in the lives of others, whether good or bad. At least at times, to someone else we are a leader. Fully realizing that God holds the reins of our heart should have an overwhelming influence on our hospitality and generosity toward others. What actions flowing from our heart demonstrate humility?

> "But whoever has this world's goods and sees his brother in need, and shuts up his **heart** from him, how does the love of God abide in him. My little children, let us not *love* in word or tongue, but in deed and in truth." I JOHN 3:17-18

Our heart empowers us to reach out to others, putting our words into action that is if our heart is filled with the love of God. You have probably observed many generous people who openly denied a place for God anywhere in their life, let alone in their heart. I certainly do not want to sound judgmental or harsh, but it is not uncommon for some people of "means" to show off their wealth and assure their own hearts before others by extending a helping hand. It makes them feel good! But true generosity, from the heart, is not how it makes us feel but rather how it encourages the hearts of others. A true leader has the love of God in their heart and it flows unencumbered. But how can we be sure and know with certainty? How can we know that our heart is right toward God? Can we be certain that our motives are not selfish?

> "And by this we know that we are of the *truth*, and shall assure our **hearts** before Him, for if our **heart** condemns us God is greater than our **heart** and knows all things. Beloved if our **heart** does not condemn us, we have confidence toward God. I John 3:19-21

There is a lot of "heart" in these verses. We have all experienced a sense of condemnation, but perhaps were not aware that its source was in our own heart. It is not other people that truly condemn us; it is our own heart. Many have been literally weighed down with condemnation, for one reason or another, even for long periods of time. Perhaps that condemnation continues to this day. The heart is powerful, what can you do? The good news of the gospel is this: "God is greater than our heart". God has created great power in our hearts, but that power is not greater than He who created it—God! What a wonderful realization this is, to know with certainty that God is just a prayer away from cleansing our hearts and putting himself back on the throne of our lives. His throne is in our hearts and He remains in control- Praise God! Because "God knows all things", and reveals the word of truth to our hearts, as we are sensitive to hear His voice confirmed in holy Scripture; we can have "confidence toward God" experiencing freedom and the joy of the Lord.

> "And whatever we ask we receive from Him, because we keep His commandments and do those things that are pleasing in His sight. And this is His commandment that we should believe on the name of His Son Jesus Christ and

> love one another as He gave us commandment.
> I John 3:22-23

This Scripture is a fitting transition to the next chapter which focuses on prayer. One aspect of prayer is simply asking God for the answers to questions and pressing needs that challenge us daily. We can expect a specific response from God when we consistently practice obedience to His commands. We simply need to follow His instructions. He makes His will abundantly clear in Scripture. Living by the power of God's word in our life brings pleasure to God.

Several years ago I preached on the subject of pleasing God. The Bible is clear that this is not only possible, but probable. I was surprised by the response of some older mature Christians that were totally unaware that this was possible. It caught me off guard. Were they indicating that pleasing God is not humanly possible? I hope that was not their thinking. I am certain that their hearts knew better. The commandment spoken of here is to "*believe* on the name of His Son Jesus Christ". Many years earlier they had made the confession of faith unto salvation found in Romans 10:9. They confessed with their mouth the Lord Jesus and *believed in their heart* that God had raised Him from the dead. That confession continues to please God today, giving every believer the confidence of answered prayer.

Ponder this in your Heart

Your heart has the potential of tremendous influence. The apostle John makes the point that "God is greater than our heart". How does the vastness of God's power influence your understanding of the human heart?

CHAPTER EIGHT | The Heart and Prayer

There are practices in the Christian life that through repetition should become habits. Obviously, these are good habits that create a deeper fellowship with Christ. Prayer should be at the top of the list, along with fasting and Bible meditation. Scripture often links prayer and fasting together. In the Sermon on the Mount, Jesus said that prayer and fasting done properly would receive God's reward. "But you, when you pray, go into your room, and when you have shut your door, pray to your Father who is in the secret place; and your Father who sees in secret will reward you openly. But you when you *fast*, anoint your head and wash your face, so that you do not appear to men to be *fasting*, but to your Father who is in the secret place; and your Father who sees in secret will *reward* you openly" (Matthew 6:6,17-18). These disciplines interact with the heart. They influence the heart and are influenced by the heart.

> "Rejoice in the Lord always; again I will say, rejoice! Let your forbearing spirit be known to all men. The Lord is near. Be anxious for nothing, but in everything by prayer and supplication with thanksgiving let your requests be made known to God. And the peace of God which surpasses all comprehension shall *guard* your **hearts** and your minds in Christ Jesus." PHILIPPIANS 4:4-7

One of the many rewards of prayer is peace and an absence of anxiety. That is a big reward. Let's break this verse down into bite size morsels to get the full meaning. That in essence is Scripture meditation; chewing repeatedly on the key words of a verse until we have digested its meaning. The first step in prayer is to "rejoice". Rejoice means to experience joy and gladness with exhilaration. It is a pleasurable outward expression, even to the extent of shouting. But in this context we are to "rejoice in the Lord". Our first expression in prayer is to openly and enthusiastically declare the joy of the Lord. Let the world know you enjoy Christ. Note that the command to "rejoice" is repeated; it is of double importance. We may be entering prayer with a sad heart; but none the less, this is where we begin. Starting in this manner will engage our heart; where joy is at home.

"Forbearing" is ceasing or restraining from action and eliciting patience and long suffering. It is to be a visible expression, "known to all men". Many find it difficult to witness for Christ. At least they are confused on how to share Christ with others. If the "joy of the Lord" is in your heart, then let it out for the world to see. What could be more natural than to "let your light so shine before men" (Matthew 5:16).

The assurance that "the Lord is near" lays a powerful ground work for the eradication of anxiety, through the power of prayer. Knowing that the Lord is always with us, elicits the faith we need in all circumstances. If we are not to be anxious about anything; a full understanding of what this means is essential. In the original Greek the word "anxious" has a much deeper meaning than to worry. It means to nurture worry by brooding over something like a mother hen broods over her chicks. It is over thinking a situation causing it to swell up beyond its proper size. As a parent and husband, I like many others tend to worry when a loved one does not return home on time. If a member of my family is supposed to be home at 11 PM and the clock advances to 11:15, I begin over thinking. For the next several minutes I begin forming vivid pictures in my mind of what could have happened to them, usually an automobile accident. By 11:30 I am making a phone call, and if I do not get the relief I am seeking it just takes 15 more minutes and I am headed for my car. That it usually when they drive in the driveway. Quite honestly, since I have grown in my understanding of the heart and allow it to take the lead over my wandering and over-activated mind, anxiety is much less of an issue in my life. Anxiety can take many forms and apply to a multitude of situations. You can over- think a project, a comment from a friend, a past or future event; you name it. Give your mind a rest and let your heart take control. The mind works poorly when the heart is not in charge.

In several places in Matthew 6:25-38, Jesus emphasizes the importance of overcoming anxiety. Depression is suffered by many people today in our country. Anxiety and depression go hand in hand. "Anxiety in the *heart* of man causes depression, but a good word makes it glad" (Proverbs 12:25). The battle is in the heart. The most accurate understanding of "anxious" in these verses is "to take no thought". In this passage Christ uses the term five times, instructing us not to be anxious about the everyday concerns of life. We are to "take no thought" about food and drink, or how we are going to pay for our clothing. We are not to over-think potential future problems or how long we might live. The best way not to over- think is to allow our heart to take control. God does His greatest work in our heart. The mind tends to wonder off at an inordinate pace and will not come to a place of equilibrium until it follows the calming rhythm of the heart, most certainly a heart filled with Spirit of God. The way we give the heart opportunity to take control is to take our requests to God in prayer; asking Him, in a spirit of gratefulness to supply our needs. When this happens God promises us His peace; a peace far beyond that which our mind is capable of understanding. It is a place where our heart and mind are secure — in Christ Jesus.

I have just illustrated Scripture "meditation" by focusing on individual words in a verse at a pace which allows for repetition. Chewing on Scripture like a cow chews on grass. Let's take a look at some Scriptures that teach the importance of meditation.

> "This book of the law shall not depart from your mouth, but you shall meditate in it day and night, that you may observe to do according to all that is written in it. For then you will make your way prosperous, and then you will have good success.
> JOSHUA 1:8

Moses had just died and his assistant Joshua was receiving instruction from the Lord. He was instructed to be strong and courageous as they entered the Promised Land to take it as their own possession. This would all be possible if he stayed obedient to God's commandments, meditating on them "day and night". How does someone meditate in the night? Is God asking Joshua to stay awake and lose important sleep? I do not believe that is what He is asking. The answer is found in Psalms 119:11. "Your word I have hidden in my *heart*, that I might not sin against You." Scripture residing in the heart requires no conscious mental effort to bring it to remembrance. God is just as eager to supply our needs in our sleep as during the waking hours; "... for He gives to His beloved even in his sleep" (Psalm 127:2 NASV). Joshua was promised success and prosperity. I believe most people desire success and prosperity. It would be even more enjoyable if we allowed God to define these terms for us. Prosperity and success encompass far more than just money and popularity. Nonetheless, this promise is for anyone who makes God the Lord of their life, whole heartedly purposing to do His will. This all came to pass in Joshua's life as years later he received the land promised him while still enjoying the vigor of a young man at the advanced age of eighty five. This command to meditate on the Word of God was not only directed to Joshua, but to anyone willing to trust their life to the Lord. What God does for others He will do for you! We find a similar admonition for everyone in Psalms 1:1-2. "Blessed is the man who walks not in the counsel of the ungodly, nor stands in the path of sinners, nor sits in the seat of the scornful; but his delight is in the law of the Lord, and in His law he *meditates day and night*". God's word is law and when it is obeyed it brings great reward and blessing. God's commandments are not designed to be a continual reminder that He is in charge. They exist to provide a way in which we can discover and enjoy an abundant life, guarding us from the destruction of evil people who disdain the Lord and His statutes. But where does the "heart" fit in all of this? The following verses will provide the answer.

> "I call to remembrance my song in the night; I *meditate* within my **heart**, and my spirit makes diligent search." PSALMS 77:6

I discussed earlier, the rejoicing of the heart. This falls in the category of "meditation". Meditating also means to talk to ourselves, or to murmur or mutter. But it is not just talking under your breath, it also can involve singing. This verse points out that speaking and singing to ourselves takes place in the *heart*. Often, meditation is a celebration of song in our heart. In the original Hebrew there is the additional understanding that the sound in our heart is like the sound of a harp when struck, or the cooing of a dove, the sighing of men. In the King James Version of the Bible "meditate" here is translated "commune". Using this term affords us added understanding of what is happening in our heart. This type of exchange within ourselves is very private and precious.

> "Let the words of my mouth and the *meditation* of my **heart** be acceptable in your sight, O Lord, my strength and my redeemer." PSALMS 19:14

> "My mouth shall speak wisdom, and the *meditation* of my **heart** shall give understanding." PSALMS 49:3

I believe Scripture teaches that "meditation" takes place when the truth of God's word transitions from our mind and enters our heart. The heart then expresses this truth in word, song, or thought. This may culminate in prayer when the heart communes with God in response to this soul-changing encounter with His truth.

The mouth speaks "wisdom", and the "understanding" occurs in the heart. The wisdom comes from the heart and goes full circle, because "out of the abundance of the heart, the mouth speaks". Christ also said to "settle it in your *hearts* not to meditate beforehand on what you will answer" (Luke 21:14). This was His instruction to believers who might experience future persecution. They were not to think and plan out in advance how they were to react, but trust Christ to provide wisdom when the need arose. Decisions made from the heart afford us the peace that only Christ can supply.

"Fasting" is another Christian discipline that has a connection with our heart. As mentioned earlier it is often accompanied by prayer. Prayer and fasting go hand in hand. Fasting takes our minds off food and other earthly pursuits so we can gain a stronger spiritual focus.

> "But as for me, when they were sick, my clothing was sackcloth; I humbled myself with fasting; and my prayer would return to my own **heart**."
> PSALMS 35:13

In this Psalm King David sets a great example of crying out to God when the enemy rises up to pull you down. David was often at war, whether for his country, or for himself personally. He knew that humility was a necessity for victory and fasting and prayer were essential in making it a reality in his life and immediate circumstances. The results he was seeking from the Lord were often painfully slow in coming. Most of us can identify with this type of challenge on our patience. Many years ago I spent a great deal of time studying prayer. I read several

tremendous books on the subject, written by mighty men of God. I scoured the Scriptures and made it a point to listen to teachers and pastors who were well versed and practiced in the subject. And of course, I purposed to pray often with diligence and sincerity. One of the key points I learned was that prayer was a circle of communication, beginning with God, received by the believer and then sent back to Him. I first had to silence my own voice and the voice of the enemy, and then ask God to speak clearly to me so that I would know His will. This was especially true of intercessory prayer. If I was to know who to pray for, and how to pray, then it was imperative to know who and what was on the heart of God, and how He wanted me to pray. In this passage, it is interesting that the prayer of David "returned" to his *heart*. Initially, he had to have the prayer in his heart if there was any possibility of it returning to that location. To me this is one of many indications that prayer and fasting involve the heart. Our goal should be to learn to pray with our heart.

> "Now, therefore, says the Lord, 'turn to Me with all your **heart**, with fasting, with weeping, and with mourning.' So rend your **heart**, and not your garments; return to the Lord your God, for he is gracious and merciful, slow to anger, and of great kindness; and He relents from doing harm." JOEL 2:12-13

This Scripture is a reminder that we are to do the will of God with "all" our heart. A half-hearted effort will not produce satisfactory results. A whole-hearted effort is evidenced by "*fasting*, with weeping, and with mourning". My endeavor to communicate the scriptural truths of the heart has not been without resistance. I believe this is a timely message for many believers today. Learning to live the Christian life by the empowered heart is a transforming experience that I believe God desires for His children. Satan is not interested in us becoming more like Jesus Christ.

In this past year I have been physically, emotionally, and spiritually exhausted at the hands of the enemy. There is nothing special about me; but God has made it clear that as Christians "we do not wrestle against flesh and blood, but against principalities, against powers, against the rulers of the darkness of this age, against spiritual hosts of wickedness in heavenly places" (Ephesians 6:12). On several occasions I have experienced uncontrollable "weeping", stronger than any time in my life. I was not in control of the weeping, God was, and it was from my heart. I believe I understand what it is to "rend your heart".

When I was ten years old we moved to a small logging area in Oregon. We lived in a small but comfortable home in the woods. Dad traveled several miles each day to attend classes at a Bible college in Eugene, while mom drove several miles in the opposite direction to teach in a small rural school. Our home on a five acre parcel on top of a hill, in the midst of the forest, had several outbuildings; one of which was a dynamite shack. I had never seen a building like this before. It was not large, approximately eight feet by twelve feet and eight feet high. But it was built with large rough sawn boards stacked flat, one on top of the other. It was constructed to withstand tremendous force. If the dynamite stored therein was to ignite, none of it would be expected to escape the building. Dynamite is very useful in blowing things apart. That is exactly the picture which describes "to rend". It means to separate any substance into pieces with tremendous force, like dynamite. This is a powerful Scripture describing the actions of a vigorous heart, a weeping heart turned to God in fasting and mourning; the sorrow of which reduces it to pieces, resulting in a broken heart, a heart condition that Christ experienced on the cross. God says He dwells "with him who has a contrite and humble spirit, to revive the heart of the contrite ones" (Isaiah 57:15). God works miracles with a heart renewed by Him.

> "So Jesus answered and said to them. Have faith in God. For assuredly, I say to you, whoever says to this mountain, 'be removed and be cast into the sea', and does not *doubt* in his **heart**, but *believes* that those things he says will be done, he will have whatever he says. Therefore I say to you, whatever things you ask when you *pray, believe* that you receive them and you will have them. And whenever you stand *praying,* if you have anything against anyone, *forgive* him that your Father in heaven may also *forgive* your trespasses. But if you do not *forgive* neither will your Father in heaven *forgive* your trespasses.
> Mark 11:22-26

There are several key terms in this portion of Scripture, that working together unleash the power of prayer. They are "faith", "believe", "forgive", and "heart". Moving mountains by beseeching God is a huge example of answered prayer used in this text. Can we ask God anything and automatically receive it? No, there is much more to it than that. But we can have the faith that moves mountains. We can have the substance of faith that prays big prayers and receives big answers. The term that links all the others into one cohesive reality is "heart". We learned in the tenth chapter of Romans that the "word of faith" is in the heart. We also know that out of the abundance of the heart the "mouth speaks". The apostle Mark in this Scripture quotes Jesus as saying we must have this faith "in God" and not to "doubt" in our *heart*. Doubting is the opposite of "believing" and God instructs us to believe on Christ in our *heart*. Faith that gives prayer its substance is found in the heart, not in the mind. The example of prayer discussed here does not come from the intellect, it flows from the heart; that is a heart free of doubt and full of faith in believing.

But yet there is one more essential ingredient that makes a heartfelt prayer effective. The heart must be free of unforgiveness if mountains are to be removed. Matthew 18:35 teaches that we must forgive from the "heart". The mind finds it very difficult to forgive as it races off in every direction remembering in detail the physical or emotional trauma that was experienced. But if we allow the heart to take the lead as God intended, forgiveness will be full and complete. Leviticus 19:17 says that "you shall not hate your brother in your *heart*..." I am not suggesting that we hate anyone in our mind; but the simple truth is that real hate takes place in the heart. Martin Luther was quoted as saying, "You can't stop birds from flying over your head, but you can keep them from building a nest in your hair". The nest building of hate takes place in the heart, not in the mind. The nest building of any sin or iniquity happens in the heart. And it is in the heart where it needs to be eradicated. A pure heart will guarantee a clean mind. During prayer, a heart and mind in this condition will naturally seek the will of God. And that is exactly how Christ taught us to pray. "Your kingdom come. Your will be done on earth as it is in heaven" (Matthew 6:10).

PONDER THIS IN YOUR HEART

Your heart is capable of improving and shaping your prayer life. Can you think of some specific ways you want to be more effective in prayer?

CHAPTER NINE | God's Temple Your Heart

> "Do you not know that you are the temple of God and that the *Spirit of God* dwells in you."
> I Corinthians 3:16

In conversation with fellow believers I often ask the following question. How would you sum up in one sentence the key point that defines a Christian? The answers are varied. One response is, "someone who has confessed their sins and received forgiveness from God". Another response is, "a person who has publicly made confession that Christ is their Lord and Savior". Still another is, "anyone who calls themselves a disciple of Christ". Another answer is, "a friend of Jesus". Another person may say, "Someone who has believed and received the Holy Spirit". I've also heard, "people who consistently study the Word of God".

In asking this question my intention is not to trap anyone into a theological argument. But I must admit that I really enjoy the response that children often give. Their most common answer is, "I'm a Christian. I gave my heart to Jesus". That is exactly what they were taught in Sunday school, and that is good teaching! I believe the Scriptures in this chapter will validate my opinion.

> "...the *mystery* which has been hidden from ages and from generations; but now has been revealed to His saints. To them God willed to make known what are the riches of the glory of this *mystery* among the Gentiles;

which is *Christ in you*, the hope of glory."
COLOSSIANS 1:26-27

As children many of us have known this "mystery". As we grew older, like many other believers, we became adept in cognitive skills. Why wouldn't we? Throughout our schooling that was what we were graded on. We learned to over-think everything. As we grew older the challenges of adult life often became overwhelming. We didn't seem to be in touch with our heart as in our younger days. Then one day we looked in the mirror and mumbled, "I'm growing older. I wish I could be like a child again, absent from all this confusion, pressure, and pain." We can, if we learn to trust God with the simple faith of a child, and put more confidence in our hearts. "Trust in the Lord with *all your heart*, and lean not on your understanding; in all your ways acknowledge Him, and He shall direct your paths" (Proverbs 1:5-6). In many ways we all need to be like children; "for such is the kingdom of heaven". The truth of the mystery is this: "Christ in you the hope of glory". Christ in you! That is, Christ is in the heart of every true believer.

> "Assuredly, I say to you, unless you are converted and become as little children, you will by no means enter the kingdom of heaven." MATTHEW 18:3

> "The kingdom of God does not come with observation; nor will they say, 'See here!' or 'See there!' For indeed, the kingdom of God *is within you*." LUKE 17:21

When speaking of salvation and eternal life, Christ often spoke of entering the kingdom of God. When Nicodemus asked Jesus to explain salvation, Christ responded by saying; "Most assuredly I say to you, unless one is born again, he cannot see the kingdom of God" (John 3:3). He went on to explain that being born again was an act of the Spirit. We understand by Scripture, many of which I will be sharing in a few moments, that Christ was teaching that the Holy Spirit indwells all believers. For many years the idea of the kingdom of God was difficult for me to grasp. Where is the kingdom of heaven? Is it just in heaven or also on earth? Does it change or is it always constant? I usually know when I have an understanding of a truth; it's when I am able to reduce it to one or two sentences. Many years ago an evangelist and preacher from South America provided the understanding I sought. In a preaching service I attended, Juan Carlos Ortiz cleared it up for me in one sentence. "The kingdom of God is wherever God rules". That covers a lot of territory. And if I allow Him to rule in my life, that includes my heart as well.

> "But this is what was spoken by the prophet Joel: 'And it shall come to pass in the last days, says God, that I will pour out of *My Spirit* on all flesh; your sons and your daughters shall prophesy, your young men will see visions, your old men shall dream dreams'." ACTS 2:16-17

Christ always fulfills His promises. Before His crucifixion and subsequent ascension into Heaven, Christ promised that He would send the Comforter, the Holy Spirit. "But when the Comforter is come, whom I will send unto you from the Father, even the Spirit of truth, which proceedeth from the Father, He shall testify of me: And ye shall bear

God's Temple Your Heart

witness, because ye have been with me from the beginning" (John 15:26-27 KJV). More often than not, the fulfillment of God's promises seems to take considerably more time than anticipated. The apostles along with other believers were waiting in an upper room for the promise of the Holy Spirit. They had been there many days when a mighty wind filled the entire house. They were all filled with the Holy Spirit and spoke in languages they had never spoken before. Foreigners from all over Asia were there in Jerusalem for the Passover celebration. Everyone heard the "wonderful works of God" in their native language. God fulfilled His promise that they would "bear witness" of Him when the Holy Spirit empowered them. And that same promise remains today for all believers. "And I will pray the Father, and He will give you another Helper, that He may *abide* with you forever—the Spirit of Truth, whom the world cannot receive, because it neither sees Him nor knows Him, but you know Him, for He *dwells* with you and will be *in* you" (John 14:16-17).

What an amazing promise! The day will come, when God will send His Spirit, the Spirit of Christ, and He will dwell with us; not just with us, but inside each of us who know Him. God's promises come to those who wait in hope. We stand on the escalator of life, each moment getting closer and closer to heaven. Each forward movement of life brings us into contact with future events foretold in the Scriptures. Many of us have stood and even walked on those moving pathways at airport terminals. Much like life, when you step on one, things go by very fast, speeding you to your destination, the gate and then the plane that scoops you up into the air. You can be certain that the day is coming when you will meet Christ face to face; but not until you have fulfilled your calling as His "witness". And the power to be that "witness" is only possible by the empowering of the Holy Spirit.

> "He who believes in Me, as the Scripture has said, out of his **heart** will flow rivers of living water. But this He spoke concerning the Spirit whom those believing in Him would receive; for the *Holy Spirit* was not yet given, because Jesus was not yet glorified." JOHN 7:38-39

The apostle John tells us exactly where the Holy Spirit resides. He sets up shop right in the center of our soul, directly in the middle of our being—the heart. Why is this important? Simply put, because it is God's plan. The heart is where God does His work, a powerful work which flows out of us as a witness to the world of His great power and love. As we have seen over and over again in Scripture God emphasizes the heart, not the mind. I am not ignoring the fact that the mind is of great importance. We are instructed to have the "mind of Christ". The mind and heart are designed to work together, with the heart taking the lead. The empowerment which makes this possible is the presence of the Holy Spirit in our heart. This power is not stagnant; it flows continuously. Abusing and misusing it can dam it up. If you will, picture in your mind a clear and powerful flowing river, high in the mountains. As you walk along the edge it gradually begins to narrow. Erosion has caused debris to slide into the river. Eventually larger limbs and branches are joined by logs. The flow slows and narrows, becoming dark and murky and in danger of being completely choked off by a log jam. What can we do? We blow up the log jam with dynamite. Sin, which grieves the Holy Spirit, can gradually erode and narrow the flow of His power in our heart. Letting it continue until a log jam occurs is a horrible thought. That is exactly why we are admonished to "guard" our hearts. What do we do? We blow up the log jam with dynamite, the dynamite of humble prayer which renders or breaks up our proud heart.

> "Now He who establishes us with you in Christ and has anointed us in God, who also has sealed us and given us the *Spirit* in our **hearts** as a guarantee." II CORINTHIANS 1:21-22

The life we receive from God as believers seems too good to be true, but God has done a work in our hearts to "establish" this truth. God has placed His Spirit in our hearts as a "guarantee" that our past, present, and future are held firmly in God's hand. This is a pledge from God, much like earnest money given at the beginning of a transaction for surety that the money will, at a future date, be paid in full. To be established in Christ means that we are unmistakably immovable in Him. Like a soldier in the battle field, we are securely dug in. We are "anointed" (touched and consecrated) by God, thereby being fully equipped to fulfill His calling as a soldier of Christ. We have put on His armor; we have put on Christ. It is an irrefutable fact that we belong to God and are supernaturally equipped to carry out His work on earth. The Holy Spirit assures us of the reality of these truths being "sealed" in our heart. "Sealed" is a key word in the seventh chapter of Revelation. Twelve thousand from each of the twelve tribes of Israel are listed as being "sealed" at the end of the age. "Do not harm the earth,

A Smarter Heart

the sea, or the trees till we have sealed the servants of our God on their foreheads." In the past I have been tempted to think that I was missing out by not being included with the twelve thousands in this special touch of God. But I know better now, being fully assured years ago that I was "sealed" by God receiving the guarantee of the Holy Spirit in my heart. "The Spirit Himself bears witness with our spirit that we are children of God" (Romans 8:16). There should absolutely be no question that we belong to God. The witness that we are His children rests deeply in our hearts; we need only tap into it. The heart is at the center of our faith in Christ. As we progress in confessing Christ as Lord, we will continue to live in His presence, and enjoy making Him known to all.

> "And because you are sons, God has sent forth the *Spirit* of His Son into your **hearts** crying out, 'Abba Father!'" GALATIANS 4:6

It needs to be repeated. God repeats it many times in Scripture. God Himself placed the Spirit of Christ into our hearts. The Holy Spirit IS the Spirit of Christ. The apostles were grieved by the thought of Jesus leaving them, but He made it clear that He was going to do something truly unbelievable after His departure. He had walked with and beside them in the past; now He would dwell within them, and within any who would put their faith in Him, and make Him Lord of their life.

"Abba" is the Hebrew word for "father". The Spirit of Christ within our hearts screams out Father, Father! We enjoy the intimate fellowship with God that only a loving father and child can experience. The Spirit of God in our

God's Temple Your Heart

heart understands things that are beyond our comprehension. Because of our weakness the "Holy Spirit Himself makes intercession for us with groanings which cannot be uttered. (Romans 8:26). There is a very tight union between the Holy Spirit and Christ, and that alliance is lived out in our heart. And Christ who "searches the hearts knows what the mind of the Spirit is, because He makes intercession for the saints according to the will of God. (Romans 8:27). This is a union which includes God, and we are brought into that union. This fellowship that we enjoy is with the Father, Son, and Holy Spirit. The Spirit of Christ, knowing the will of God, cries out to God on our behalf. We can be assured a prayer of that nature is completely pure and powerful. It is difficult for me to express how intimately I am acquainted with that truth. Not many months ago I was experiencing a deep spiritual struggle. It was not a wavering of belief but rather a birthing of greater faith and purpose. I was completely exhausted in the struggle, but in it became explicitly aware that Christ was personally standing before my heavenly father, making an appeal on my behalf. In the past, I had understood in my mind this hope of Christ interceding to God for me. But now, I not only knew it in my heart, but I also became aware that it was taking place in my heart. It released within me a torrent of sobbing and an awareness of deep, penetrating relief and rest. Thank God for what He accomplishes in the human heart. It is simply a miracle!

> "Now hope does not disappoint, because the *love* of God has been poured out in our **hearts** by the Holy Spirit who was given to us."
> ROMANS 5:5

Throughout recent decades a great harm has been done to the body of Christ by the ongoing argument of what constitutes the evidence of the Holy Spirit in the believer's life. The fault lies on both sides of the argument. One side has at times come close to excluding any manifestation of the Holy Spirit in our dispensation, thus nearly denying the Holy Spirit's existence at all. The other side has become so engrossed with the signs and gifts of the Holy Spirit that it has ignored the importance of knowing and heeding Him personally. Both sides have thus limited the expression of the love of God in their hearts. Chapters twelve and fourteen of I Corinthians are devoted to instruction concerning the gifts, ministries, manifestations, and offices of the Holy Spirit. To me, it is no surprise that the "love chapter" is nestled in between. We are instructed in the thirteenth chapter that even though we may possess great spiritual gifting along with tremendous qualities of character, without love we amount to nothing. We may be able to speak in other tongues, even in a heavenly language and have "all" knowledge, understanding, and faith; yet still without love we are "nothing". If we give away our entire substance to the needy and even lay down our life for others, done outside of love, there will be zero profit. What continues indefinitely is faith, hope, and love; and they are not equal, love is the greatest. The greatest thing we can possess is love. "God is love" and the Holy Spirit pours out the love of God in our heart. Can it be any wonder why God places such great importance on the heart? Allow me to be so bold as to say, that what believers need in our day is a fresh baptism of love. "By this all will know that you are My disciples, if you have *love* for one another" (John 13:35). God is all powerful! His love is all powerful! "*Love* never fails" (I Corinthians 13:8). This unfailing and all powerful love from God fills our heart and flows from our heart as a work of the Holy Spirit of God in our heart. That is a mouth full. No, it is a heart full!

> "For this reason I bow my knees to the Father of our Lord Jesus Christ, from whom the whole family in heaven and earth is named, that He would grant you, according to the riches of His glory to be strengthened with might through *His spirit in the inner man,* that *Christ may dwell in your* **hearts** through faith; that you being rooted and grounded in *love,* may be able to comprehend with all the saints what is the width and length and depth and height—to know the *love* of Christ which passes knowledge; that you may be *filled* with all the fullness of God." EPHESIANS 3:14-18

Just how full is our heart? These verses fully answer the question. Our heart is overflowing! This portion of Scripture is pregnant with spiritual life. I implore you to purpose in your heart to meditate on it in great length. I will do my best to get you started. All three members of the Deity are mentioned in this passage. The Holy Spirit in our "inner man", Christ in our "heart", as we are "filled" with God. And why? So we can be "grounded in love". Being "rooted" in love enables us to "comprehend" truth far beyond that which is normally possible; even being intimately aware of ("knowing") Christ's love. "For in Him (Christ) dwells all the fullness of the Godhead bodily; and you are complete in Him, who is the head of all principality and power" (Colossians 2:9-10). Because Christ is the fullness of God, and He inhabits our heart; we can begin to accept that the "fullness of God" occupies our being. He not only fills us, but He overflows our soul. This great work of God is fulfilled in our heart. We certainly are not God, but He fills us with overflowing love. That is a world changer! We change the world, one soul at a time; and that is exactly what His church has been about for the last two thousand years, and will be until His soon return.

> "For there are three that bear witness in heaven: the Father, the Word, and the Holy Spirit, and these three are one." I JOHN 5:7

The first chapter of John makes it clear that the "Word" is Jesus Christ and that Christ is God. "In the beginning was the Word, and the Word was with God, and the Word was God…And the Word became flesh and dwelt among us, and we beheld His glory as the only begotten of the Father, full of grace and truth" (John 1:1, 14). The third chapter of Ephesians teaches that believers are indwelt by the Father, the Son, and the Holy Spirit. Colossians, the second chapter points out that the "Godhead" is complete in Christ, even in His earthly body. This current verse in I John puts the period on the sentence. The Father, the Son, and the Holy Spirit are one entity; what we refer to as the "trinity". Ephesians 3:17 instructs us that Christ occupies our heart. The conclusion is this: the trinity dwells in my heart. If you have confessed Jesus Christ as your savior, He also abides in your heart. The Father, the Word (Christ), and the Holy Spirit each witness to "the wonderful works of God" (Acts 2:11). They each take the witness stand and affirm that they are one. And we as Christians have this witness in ourselves. "He who believes in the Son of God has the witness in himself…and this is the testimony: that "God has given us eternal life, and this life is in His Son" (I

John 5:10, 11). The Spirit of Christ abiding in our hearts testifies of our personal salvation (Romans 8:16).

One of the most difficult things to do for many believers is to share Christ with others. For many, it strikes fear in their heart. "People make me nervous." "I don't know what to say." "I just don't have that gifting." "I wish I had the time." These are common thoughts that many Christians entertain when contemplating the command of Christ to: "go into all the world and preach the gospel to every creature" (Mark 16:15). Throughout my life time I have seen a multitude of different teachings on how to witness. Some are very simple and others quite difficult, involving hours of memorization. I am not against such teaching which is designed to prepare believers to share their faith. This is an important task that is not to be taken lightly. The task may seem daunting until we focus on God's provision to complete it. "But you shall receive *power* when the Holy Spirit has come upon you; and you *shall be witnesses* to Me in Jerusalem, and in all Judea and Samaria, and to the end of the earth" (Acts 1:8). The truth is this: more than being called "to" witness, we "are" witnesses. The power to live openly before man by letting your light shine is made possible by the Holy Spirit dwelling in your heart. He has taken up residence in your heart. Allow Him to manifest Himself to others through you. This can become a very natural way of living your life. Have you heard the phrase; "you can read him like a book". It is not always meant to be a compliment, but you can take it as one, when you are reminded of II Corinthians 3:2,3. "You are our epistle written in our *hearts*, known and read by all men; *clearly you are an epistle* of Christ, ministered by us, written not with ink but by the Spirit of the living God, not on tablets of stone but on tablets of flesh, that is of the *heart*". If you truly want to be a witness of Christ, just allow your heart to speak. Allow your heart to communicate the love of Christ.

I am not necessarily an outgoing person. I am a little introspective by nature. But that which comes natural for me is not always what is best for others. One time my wife and I were waiting in an airport preparing to board a plane for Dallas, Texas to visit our daughter and her family. Like others, we were excited and eager to enter the plane and get on our way. Then over the loudspeaker came the news. "Flight 642 has been cancelled due to mechanical failure. If you are a passenger on this flight would you please approach the flight counter?" I went to the counter along with a swarm of other passengers. The true colors of many began to shine brightly, but not so lovely. I remember the man in front of me as if it were yesterday; and I am sure the attendant does as well. This middle aged man literally blasted the young lady with His caustic remarks. The shame of her to inconvenience him was the attitude he vented. He would not stop; she was on the edge of bursting into tears. She was already under tremendous pressure trying to reschedule a large group of people, each with their own problems and agendas. Well, she survived him just in time to encounter me. For some reason I was in a good mood, and quite calm. I was nice to her! God was shining from my heart. As we talked she began to experience God's warmth. When she was through rescheduling our flight, the tears began to well up, but they were happy tears. She was calmer now. Looking me in the eye with an expression of gratitude, she shared her heart, "I will remember you as long as I live". Please do not get me wrong. I am not bragging. My past record does not have many examples of such patience and kindness. But I was quite aware why this change was occurring in my life. God was teaching me about the "heart" from His word; and it was changing me from the inside out. Inside my heart - that is. Too often, we live too small. Living large is being kind and demonstrating love to others, even those who rub us the wrong way. The best witnessing most of us can perform is simply being nice! As Christ said, "Do unto others as you would have them do unto you".

> "Come to Me, all you who labor and are heavy laden, and I will give you rest. Take My yoke upon you and learn from Me, for I am *gentle* and *lowly* in **heart** and you will find rest for your soul. For my yoke is easy and My burden is light." MATTHEW 11:28-30

Recently a very good friend of mine was excited to point out some Scriptures which talked about the heart of God. I asked him why the idea of God having a heart was a new idea to him. "I don't know," he retorted. "I guess I have always thought that a heart was only characteristic of humans. My friend is a very intelligent man, who like many of us had not given the topic much attention. There are only a few Scriptures which specifically speak of God's heart, but there are many verses which provide us with an understanding of Christ's heart. By experiencing the heart of Christ we come to know the heart of God. Colossians 2:9 makes that clear. "For in Him (Christ) dwells all the fullness of the Godhead bodily." For me personally, after studying hundreds of verses on the heart, Christ's heart takes on added meaning. The heart of Christ is the heart that God gives every believer. We know this to be true because Christ dwells in our heart. What is the nature of this unfathomable gift? It is humility at a depth that only the heart can know. The heart of Christ is "gentle" ("meek" KJV) and "lowly". The clearest way to understand meekness is to know its opposite; which is being harsh, rude, and abrupt. This type of person is inflexible to the needs and opinions of others; and rarely omits wrong doing. "Lowly" literally means to defer servilely to others or to take the posture of a slave even though that is not your position. Christ best exemplified this quality when he allowed men under his reign to hang him on a cross. This level of humility ("meek" and "lowly") is only attributed to Christ, yet as believers we are instructed to procure this sort of humility. "But sanctify the Lord God in your *hearts*, and always be ready to give a defense to everyone who asks you a reason for the hope that is in you, with *meekness* and *fear*" (I Peter 3:15). Fear in this context means reverence and respect. Peter continues on in his instruction. "Likewise you younger people, submit yourselves to your elders. Yes, all of you be submissive to one another, and be clothed with *humility*, for 'God resists the proud, but gives grace to the *humble*'" (I Peter 5:5). This grace, this unmerited empowering takes place in the heart.

    How do we receive and behave and walk in this level of grace? We accomplish it by following the instruction of Christ, to come to Him even as we struggle in our "labor". The literal and verbatim rendering of verse twenty eight in Matthew eleven is as follows. "Come hither to Me, all the you *tiring yourselves* and having been laden…". We have brought the exhaustion on ourselves by working in our own strength. When we come to Christ he desires to calm and quiet us so we can recover from our fatigue. The heart that Christ gives us is a resting heart of calmness that renews our strength. This is especially important to grasp as we enter into the next chapter of this study. It has been a long time coming, but the ground work had to be laid. The "heart" is at the center of our soul, and in the midst of everything we say and do. It must be guarded and kept at all cost. How then, in very practical ways, do we accomplish this daunting task?

PONDER THIS IN YOUR HEART

The Spirit of Christ dwells in the heart of each and every true believer. Contemplate how that one fact alone can revolutionize your life.

CHAPTER TEN | Keeping Your Heart

BACK TO THE BEGINNING

The importance of understanding and implementing the connection between the mind and the body for optimum health has been a focus of medicine for over fifty years, and yet it is only recently that it has become accepted by mainstream medicine. The study by modern science and medicine of the association between brain intelligence and heart intelligence has been pursued for at least two decades and may take many more years before it is accepted by the elite of science and medicine. The current study of the heart/brain connection known as Neurocardiology is worldwide in its scope. There are centers of study located around the globe. A significant leader in the study of the science of the heart is the *Institute Of HeartMath* located in Boulder Creek, California. They have made tremendous strides in educating people on how to manage their emotions by synchronizing communications between the brain and the heart. They use a simple method of proper breathing through the heart and additional tools such as "Inner-ease technique", "Quick Coherence Technique", and "Intelligent Energy Self-regulation".

The truth that the heart thinks is well known in science today. The heart and brain communicate, and between the two the heart sends the most information. The heart is much more than just a pump. The heart generates two independent and interworking fields of energy, electric, and magnetic. It is the largest source of electromagnetic energy in the body. The brain's electromagnetic field is not nearly as powerful. These energy systems involve four basic areas of our life: physical, emotional, mental, and spiritual. The following Scripture is an example of the numerous times that Scripture addresses differing facets of our being. "You shall love the Lord with all your *heart,* with all your soul, and with all your strength" (Deuteronomy 6:5). Learning to have consistent control over our mental thought patterns and emotions will produce profound improvement in our quality of life. The publications and videos available through the *Institute of HeartMath* can provide tremendous assistance along these lines. The intent of this study, in which we are now engaged, is to place significant attention on what the Bible teaches concerning the great mysteries of the heart. The Bible is light years ahead of science. Obviously, God knew all along what science is now discovering. In Scripture we are admonished to "guard our hearts", and if all we did was care for our physical and emotional heart, it would be of some benefit now. But by understanding and abiding by the truth of Scripture, all facets of the heart: physical, emotional, mental, and spiritual can be strengthened and protected with benefits both now and eternally. How this is accomplished may be much simpler than you think.

> "My son, give attention to my words, incline your ear to my sayings. Do not let them depart from your eyes. Keep them in the midst of your **heart,** for they are life to those who find them and *health* to all their flesh. *Keep* your **heart** with all

> diligence for out of it spring the issues of *life*. Put away from you a deceitful mouth and put perverse lips far from you. Let your eyes look straight ahead and your eyelids look right before you. Ponder the path of your feet and let your ways be established. Do not turn to the right or the left. Remove your foot from evil." PROVERBS 4:20-27

As was pointed out earlier, this is the pivotal portion of Scripture in the study of the heart. The first portion of this passage outlines the importance of the heart and motivates us to follow the central admonition to "keep" our heart diligently. The latter verses of this passage provide some very practical ways to keep the heart. In essence these eight verses sum up the entire study. Additional verses will be discussed, as they provide further insight and clarity.

The words of God are best stored in the heart, not in the mind. I am not saying that the mind is ignored in the process, quite the contrary. We are instructed to have the "mind of Christ". But communion with Christ starts in the heart which then influences us to correct thinking; bringing the mind in step with the heart. When our heart fully accepts truth from God, our entire being, soul, body, and spirit benefit. If what God communicates to us is kept in the very center of our heart we will experience true living, a quality of life which only God Himself can supply. A heart containing the commands of Christ is a healthy heart. "A sound heart is life to the body" (Proverbs 14:30). This truth is emphasized again by King Solomon in Proverbs 3:1-2. "My son do not forget my law, but let your heart keep my commands; for length of day and long life and peace they will add to you". A heart filled with truth from God is a healthy heart which promises life and health "to all their (our) flesh". We can enjoy healing for every area of the body, knowing that a sound heart makes it possible. Of course we will get ill, perhaps deathly sick, but if there is to be any healing the focal point will be the power of God abiding in the heart. The heart is the source of life and health. That is more than enough import to motivate each of us to guard it diligently.

In these verses found in chapter four of proverbs the word "keep" means to tend to our heart as a vine dresser would care for his vineyard with a design that it flourishes and grows strong. This admonition of God is in the "imperative" tense, emphasizing that it is not optional and requires immediate attention. Adding the emphasis to be "diligent" makes the assignment of first priority. It becomes the most important of all endeavors. Nothing is of any importance until this command to "keep" the heart is initiated. God is charging each of us to accept and function in the position of a guardian or ward over our heart. This commission is to be done at all times, day and night. Why? Because the heart is the fountain head of our physical, emotional, intellectual, and spiritual life!

How Is This Accomplished?

Verses twenty four through twenty seven of this chapter provide an outline of major principles, that if adhered to, will erect a solid foundation for continual success in perfecting and sustaining a healthy, stable and vibrant heart. These are principles of action, not just a way of thinking. These principles are meant to be lived out in our lives. It goes beyond just thinking differently but living differently. God makes this all possible by His grace which gives us both the desire and the power to do His will—to live a Godly life. The way we live affects the health in every aspect of our heart. And a healthy heart establishes the quality of our life. Verse twenty four charges us to get rid of a "deceitful" mouth. Remember that out of the "abundance of the heart the mouth speaks". It is a two way street. A devious mouth pollutes the heart and a polluted heart speaks out deceit. What then is "deceit"? In the context of this verse, "deceitful" means out of control. A deceitful mouth is out of control, it resists outside constraints.

I remember the first time my family visited relatives in southern California. I was just ten years old having spent my early years enjoying a rural farm lifestyle. A trip to Los Angeles to visit aunts, uncles and cousins had the prospects of a great adventure. There was no doubt that the grandest day would be spent at Disneyland. We traveled by car from Idaho and my first encounter with freeways was quite daunting. A multitude of automobiles racing at high speeds just inches from each other. My heart raced with both fear and excitement. After a short time I actually became comfortable. It was easy to trust my father's driving skills, although I think he was a little unnerved himself. Watching Dad maneuver the car at high speeds planted a desire in me to drive, and to drive fast; enjoying full control of this man-made piece of machinery.

Our day at Disneyland finally came and I was to enjoy this exhilaration and freedom behind the wheel of a motor car. My cousins had prepared me ahead of time for the highlight attraction of all E-ticket rides, Autopia. We approached the scaled down freeway with appropriately sized vehicles that younger people could drive on their own. But there was one hurdle to jump. Would the top of my head reach the line on the sign? Would I make the mark? O happy day! I made it! I was behind the wheel of a shiny new miniature automobile. I had it all to myself. As I journeyed along the road I experienced a bit of a letdown. I was not in full control. You see there was a "governor" on the engine that limited the speed of the car. And there were concrete barriers that limited my lateral movement. And even worse, there was no opportunity to pass another car. But I did have fun nonetheless.

We are instructed to put a "governor" on our mouth, and "put perverse lips" far away. A "deceitful" mouth is "ungovernable" and disobedient. It is not funny to say that; "I have just washed my mouth, and I cannot do a thing with it". When I was young and made a foul remark, my mother immediately washed my mouth out with soap. Better to have soap in my stomach than to have a damaged heart.

The literal rendering of this verse is as follows: "Turn away from you pervertedness of mouth and put far from you straying lips". James 1:26 makes the issue even clearer. "If anyone among you thinks he is religious, and does not bridle his tongue but deceives his own *heart*, this one's religion is useless". These are very strong words. This is a very serious matter. A tongue out of control does great damage to the heart. The heart is the source of true religion. It is where the Spirit of God dwells and does His great work. What many see as just a bad habit actually paralyzes the heart, making it incapable of flowing freely with the life of Christ.

I will sum it up; "So then, my beloved brethren, let every man be swift to hear, slow to speak…" (James 1:19).

"Let your eyes look straight ahead and your eyelids look

right before you." Actions are often more important than words. The bottom line is that God requires that we control ourselves and when we don't, there is a price to pay. The price again is harm to our heart. There are numerable admonitions in Scripture to look straight ahead and not be distracted by evil on the left and right. This truth is magnified in the last verse of this passage. Straying eyes can only lead to evil. King Solomon instructs men not to be lured by a harlot. "Do not let your *heart* turn aside to her ways, Do not stray into her paths" (Proverbs 7:25). Immoral conduct literally harms the heart, physically and spiritually. The Apostle Paul declares this in his first letter to the church in Corinth. "*Flee* sexual immorality. Every sin that a man does is outside the body, but he who commits sexual immorality sins against his own body" (I Corinthians 6:18). A change of focus is the first action taken in straying off the path of righteousness and stepping onto a path of sin. The instruct-ion to "ponder the path of your feet" encourages us to make a plan ahead of time and follow that plan with actions that clear the way for a successful journey, one uninterrupted by painful and unnecessary detours. The word "ponder" in the original Hebrew is "piel", and means to prepare and make the way level by rolling a cylinder over the surface. In other words we are to prepare a level path to allow an unhindered route of travel to the desired goal. Jesus "steadfastly set his face to go to Jerusalem" (Luke 9:51). Christ determined well in advance that He would choose the path that led to His crucifixion. If we are going to enjoy the benefits of a pure heart as did our Lord, by His power within us, we must follow His example and "run with endurance the race that is set before us, looking unto Jesus the author and finisher of our faith, who for the joy that was set before Him endured the cross" (Hebrews 12:1-2).

When we follow the command to "let your ways be *established*" we are setting our heart on a sound foundation. This decision is made in advance as we purpose in our heart to do the will of God at any cost. In Hebrews 13:9 we are reminded that it is "good that the *heart* be *established* by grace". We must be firm and resolute in our convictions, and when we are, our heart will not waver. Start the race with the finish in mind and the joy of winning will provide the motivation to obtain the prize. During my first track and field practice, as a twelve year old, I observed the antithesis of this truth. I will never forget it! One of my classmates was competing in the 440 yard race. To try and complete the lap in sprint form is very difficult, even for the seasoned runner, let alone a twelve year old. My classmate was mature for his age and very strong. He was a tough character; therefore I concluded that he would finish with some level of success. Not so! Coming around the last corner with 100 yards of straight away ahead of him, he fell to the ground, his spirit broken, his body in pain, and sobbing in tears. Boy was I surprised! Throughout my High School track career I competed in that race along with some shorter distances. Although I was very competitive at that distance, it was my least favorite. It just plain hurt. I had to keep my eye on the finish line and remember the joy of crossing the tape first. It was a race that took a lot of heart, a strong heart that required years of practice to procure and continued discipline to maintain.

"Remove your foot from evil" is the final admonition of this portion of Scripture.

As pointed out earlier, explicit action is required to maintain a healthy heart. Evil of any sort damages the heart. Continuing in evil will ultimately destroy it. "Repentance essentially means to turn 180 degrees and go in the opposite direction; leave sin behind and seek right living. "*Flee also youthful lusts; but pursue righteousness, faith, love, peace with those who call on the Lord out of a pure heart*" (II Timothy 3:22). Seeing how close we can get to worldly living without falling head long into sin is foolishness at best. We must get as far away from a worldly lifestyle as possible. Anything less than total commitment to the ways of God will taint our heart, ultimately resulting in great destruction. We leave evil behind by seeking Godly living. A Godly life is one of faith and love and peace. A worldly life is made up of fear and uncertainty, confusion and hopelessness. A re-deemed heart knows this to be true. A pure heart will make it a reality. "So God, who knows the *heart*, acknowledged them (Gentiles) by giving them the Holy Spirit, just as He did to us (Jews), and made no distinction between us and them, *purifying* their *hearts* by faith" (Acts 15:8-9).

PSALMS THAT INFORM AND INSTRUCT

There are a multitude of Scriptures throughout the Bible that give practical insight on "how to" guard and keep our heart. Just as in the previous Scriptures, it only works if they are heeded, not just heard. "But be doers of the word, and not hearers only, deceiving yourselves" (James 1:22). At this point, the most fool-hearty thing we could do would be to deceive our own heart. It is mandatory that we take these Scriptures to heart and act on them.

> "I would have lost heart unless I had believed that I would see the goodness of the Lord in the land of the living. *Wait* on the Lord, be of good courage and He shall strengthen your **heart**. *Wait* I say on the Lord."
>
> PSALMS 27:13-14

This is just one of many Scriptures that provide practical advice on strengthening our heart on a regular basis. The first use of "heart" in this passage is not the Hebrew word "lehv" that we have been focusing on throughout this study. In the King James translation it says; "I had *fainted*". In the New American Standard translation the phrase "I would have *despaired*" is used. The clearest under-standing comes from looking at the literal rendering from early manuscripts. The Masoretic Text reads: "If I would *not faith* (steadfastly trust, and firmly adhere) to see the goodness of YHWH in the earthland of the living ones!" What then strengthens the heart? The answer lies in the hope that while we live in the here and now, in an evil world, we do not cease to believe that we will visibly see God perform His mighty acts of goodness on our behalf. Our expectation is that we anticipate this "goodness" to happen in this present day, on planet earth. That is not the testimony of the vast majority of people I talk to, whether believers in Jesus Christ or not. Quite frankly, a significant number of people are so beat down and discouraged by the evil of the world that they have lost hope. If you lose the confidence that God will ultimately exercise His redeeming power, your heart will be severely damaged. But it does not mean it is injured beyond repair.

My grandmother often used the phrase; "I've seen sicker

cats than that get well!" What was she saying? No matter how desperate our personal or collective struggle may become, it is never beyond God's ability to heal. I recently experienced a literal "sick cat" saga. While my daughter and I backed out of the garage in route to an appointment with my physician, we were startled by the presence of an injured cat in the driveway. We were familiar with this cat as it frequented our property and the neighbor's property nearby in search of food. A woman stepped out of a car parked next to our property and informed us that the cat had been hit by an automobile and she had called the county animal control department. The feline appeared to be suffering and I was sure that death was a certainty. Four days later he walked past my sliding glass door, headed for the garage with the hope of discovering some life sustaining morsels of food. I was startled, but eager to oblige. He looked the worse for wear, but had not given up the ghost. Some things just take a while to come full circle. Given enough time I am certain that this cat, that we have aptly named "Lucky" will be fully healed, perhaps even better than before. "Lucky" is a great illustration of what is needed for our hearts to be invigorated. God instructs us twice in the fourteenth verse of this passage to "wait" on the Lord. It literally means to stand firm and resolute with the expectation that God in His righteousness will intervene for good, that good will triumph over evil. This must be our perspective, believing in advance that the Lord will, in His perfect timing, make everything right. And He will! He will "strengthen your *heart.*"

> "He will not be afraid of evil tidings; his **heart** is steadfast, *trusting* in the Lord. His **heart** is established; he will not be afraid, until he sees

his desire upon his enemies."
PSALMS 112:7-8

Who is this Scripture describing? The opening verse of this chapter declares that it is the "man who fears the Lord". This is a person who has a holy and awesome respect for God; for His power, His laws, and His word. This is a child of God who is motivated to obey the Lord wholly, being careful not to stray from His will. In modern vernacular, it is a person who has great respect for the Lord. A good example is found in the life of Cornelius in Acts the tenth chapter. God used Cornelius to show Peter and the early Church that citizens of other nations also had access to God's saving grace. God's love was not limited to the Jewish people only. Scripture describes Cornelius as "a devout man and one who *feared* God with all his household, who gave alms generously to the people, and prayed to God always" (v. 2). God heard his prayers and sent an angel to visit him in a vision. Cornelius received instruction from the angel, which he obeyed, enabling Peter to bring the salvation message to him and his entire household. Because Cornelius truly feared God, He and his family and friends were established in the faith of the Lord Jesus Christ.

To be "steadfast" and "established" means to take something that may be wavering or insecure and fastening it down securely. An uncertain and vacillating heart can be likened to the "double-minded" man found in The Epistle of James. This is a man "unstable in all his ways" (v. 8). I Chronicles 12:33 introduces us to some of King David's fighting men who were not *"double-hearted"* but were able to "keep ranks". These men were able to stay in battle formation because they possessed hearts that trusted in God and therefore did not fear their enemies. That is exactly the heart described here in Psalms 112. To put it simply, a heart that trusts "in the Lord" will not waver in fear but stay firmly fixed in the "fear of the Lord". To acquire and maintain a healthy heart; we must trust God explicitly.

> "Be of good courage, and He shall strengthen your **heart**, all you who *hope* in the Lord."
> PSALMS 31:24

Being courageous is necessary to maintain a strong heart. Where does courage come from? The first chapter of Joshua profoundly answers this question. Please stop and read it now. Verse nine sums it up. "Have not I commanded you? Be strong and of good courage; do not be afraid, nor be dismayed, for the Lord your God is with you wherever you go." Don't think this promise is specific to Joshua only, remember the instruction of this Psalm to be courageous, "all you" who put their "*hope* in the Lord". This command is for everyone who believes God's promises, and carries with them the expectation of His presence and power in every situation. The Apostle Paul echoed this truth in his defense before King Agrippa. "And now I stand and am judged for the *hope* of the promise made by God to our fathers" (Acts 26:7). Paul and Joshua both stood tall in hope and courage. Courage strengthens the heart. Hope strengthens the heart. But not hope in just anything, hope that is grounded in Christ alone. The hope we have in the promise of the second coming of Christ, though not now visible, explodes from the pen of Paul in his letter to the Romans. "For we were saved in this *hope*, but *hope* that is seen is not *hope*; for why does one still *hope* for what he sees? But if we *hope* for what we do not see, we eagerly wait for it with perseverance" (Romans 8:24-25). This God ordained hope will be with us forever. Some things pass away but a few endure indefinitely. Hope, like faith and love is constantly available; it need not depart. "And now abide faith, hope, love, these three; but the greatest of these is love" (I Corinthians 13:13). Love certainly is the greatest of these three and yet love "... hopes all things..." (I Corinthians 13:7). Hope has its place, and along with faith and love, its place is in our heart.

> "Your word I have hidden in my **heart** that I might not sin against you." PSALMS 119:11

Any sin or transgression is harmful to the heart. Removing ourselves as far as possible from sin and moving closer to the heart of Christ will bring peace and joy to our souls as our heart is strengthened. This is performed by hiding the Word of God deep in our heart. Note that the text does not call us to hide the word in our mind. Although memorizing Scripture is helpful and necessary, we are encouraged to go further and plant the Word of God in our heart. This is done by "meditating"

on Scripture. Remember, this was part of the preparation Joshua received when he took over leadership at the passing of Moses. After being told to be "strong and very courageous", he was commanded to meditate on God's word. "This Book of the Law shall not depart from your mouth, but you shall *meditate* in it day and night, that you may observe to do according to all that is written in it. For then you will make your way *prosperous*, and then you will have good *success*" (Joshua 1:8). Most people desire success and prosperity. God desires this for His children, and provides the means for it becoming a reality. If our life is to flourish we must be energized by a heart filled with the word, filled with Christ, for Christ is the Word.

Meditation refreshes the heart. "*Meditate* within your heart on your bed, and be *still*" (Psalms 4:4). I often listen to the Scriptures on tape while resting. In so doing I am planting the Word of God in the center of my heart. It brings calmness to my soul as I lie in stillness before the presence of God. The heart requires rest, and the benefits are shared by our entire body. Take time to recharge your battery. Essentially your physical heart is a battery. It produces and emits an electrical force. Our spiritual heart is recharged when it meditates on the things of God. "Let the words of my mouth and the *meditation* of my *heart* be acceptable in Your sight, O Lord, my strength and my Redeemer" (Psalms 19:14). The Lord is our strength! In the fifteenth chapter of John the apostle makes it clear that we cannot accomplish anything apart from Christ. But if we meditate upon Him in our heart this union becomes great and His power in us is magnified, as our heart is enriched.

> "Reproach has broken my **heart**, and I am full of heaviness; I looked for someone to take pity, but there was none; and for comforters, but I found none." Psalms 19:19

> "The humble shall see this and be glad; and you who *seek* God, your **hearts** shall live." Psalms 19:32

There are many ways to break a heart. One of the most painful is to be falsely accused of misconduct. King David was often ridiculed and scorned and this is the context of his nineteenth psalm. I am sure that all of us have been treated with con-tempt, usually leading to disgrace. It weighs us down and breaks the human heart. The heart pain is even greater when the accusations are unfounded. The pain is nearly unbearable when the contempt is uttered from the mouth of a friend. There is no relief for this heaviness of heart until someone is found to show sympathy and provide comfort. David was unable to find such a person. Perhaps you have found yourself in the same struggle. If it happens to you, follow the example of David. Go to God and find your healing in Him. God will renew your heart. God, when given an opportunity, always heals the brokenhearted and fills them with His life. "Ask, and it will be given to you; *seek*, and you will find; knock, and it will be opened to you" (Matthew 7:7). The first step to receiving a whole heart is crying out to the Lord, our great healer.

WISDOM FROM PROVERBS

If you recall, Solomon uses the term "heart" over ninety times in the Book of Proverbs. After the tenth chapter Solomon appears to instruct those of mature intelligence and ceases from focusing entirely on young people. We are never too old to gain additional knowledge and wisdom, especially when it comes from the heart and benefits the heart.

> "He who has a deceitful **heart** finds no good, and he who has a perverse tongue falls into evil. A merry **heart** does good, like medicine, but a broken spirit dries the bones." PROVERBS 17:20, 22

Two types of hearts are contrasted in these verses; a "deceitful" heart and a "merry" heart. A "merry heart" and a "broken spirit" are also presented as opposites. A person with a deceitful heart purposely deceives and misleads others for their own gain. They cheat and defraud for the purpose of trapping unsuspecting victims. Their perverted and distorted conversation creates confusion and anxiousness in others. The perversion that they pour out on others damages their own spirit. They are evil, and their lack of virtue robs them of any good in this world. If you are to guard your heart, it is absolutely essential to remove yourself from their presence.

On the positive side, a merry heart works like medicine, providing emotional and physical healing for the entire body. Instead of dried up and lifeless bones we can enjoy energy and vitality. Remember the instruction found in the fourth chapter of Proverbs, that the Word of God hid in the heart brings life and health to our entire bodies. Please stop here and read Ezekiel chapter thirty seven, it records the Lord's instruction to Ezekiel to prophesy over the valley of dry bones. He did, and life and breath were infused into those bones and they stood on their feet. Surely God can breathe fresh life into our bodies. We have every reason to have a merry heart. God wants His children to be happy, especially in the throes of discouragement. My mom was nicknamed "happy" by her parents. Beginning as a toddler and then continuing as a child she woke up nearly every morning happy and singing. It came natural for her. For most of us it is not quite that easy. Most likely it was a gift from God. If you would like that gift from God, then ask Him. "Every good gift and every perfect gift is from above, and comes down from the Father of lights, with whom there is no variation or shadow of turning" (James 1:17).

If you are grateful for God's goodness and boundless love, then show it. Be happy, happy, happy, and you will enjoy the benefits of a merry heart.

> *"Ointment* and *perfume* delight the **heart** and
> And the sweetness of a man's friend gives
> delight by hearty counsel.*"* Proverbs 27:9

To "delight the heart" literally means to make the heart "joyful". Down-to-earth advice on how to fill the heart with joy is found in this proverb. The Scriptures are replete with instructions to anoint with oil. James 5:14 gives instruction on what our first initiative should be in combating an illness. "Is anyone among you sick? Let him call for the elders of the church, and let them pray over him, anointing him with oil in the name of the Lord." For a multitude of years it has been common knowledge that numerous oils, are very beneficial for fighting illness and maintaining optimum health. These oils come from a vast number of plants that God has provided for our benefit. The odor alone from many of these oils is uplifting. These ointments literally bring joy to the heart. A joyful heart is a healthy heart. The simple exposure to perfumes offers the same result. When the word "perfume" is used in the Old Testament it is frequently associated with "sweet". Smelling sweet things brings delight to the heart. Smells also bring back wonderful memories. The smell of pine reminds me of my summers in the mountains as a child. It also reminds me of the people I enjoyed on those vacations. The smell of peppermint reminds my wife of her grandmother who was never seen without a peppermint candy in her hand or pocket. Of all our senses the sense of smell is most closely associated with our memory.

A Smarter Heart

Odors bring back memories of the heart and mind. Simple oils and perfumes are great for guarding the heart and filling it with great joy. Never underestimate the power of the touch and smell of God's creation!

> "Hear my son and be wise and *guide* your **heart** in the way. Do not mix with wine bibbers, or with gluttonous eaters of meat. For the drunkard and the glutton will come to poverty, and drowsiness will clothe a man with rags."
> Proverbs 23:19-21

In addition to "keeping" and "guarding" our heart; we are also instructed to "guide" our heart. This is a "wise" thing to do. The foolish action to take would be to keep company with wine bibbers and gluttons. The commonality between the two is a lack of control, as this passage defines a "wine-bibber as a "drunkard". A "glutton" cannot control his eating and a "drunkard" cannot control his drinking. They are both out of control and this is damaging to the heart. But if we guide the heart away from this kind of behavior the heart will be strengthened. The word "guide" in the original Hebrew is very interesting. It clearly means to lead straight into the right way. In addition it means that the straight path leads to blessings and happiness. The right road is a straight road which leads to happiness and prosperity. The road of the glutton and drunkard is a crooked path which leads to poverty. The direct cause of this poverty is that the drunkard is often in a state of "drowsiness". The Hebrew word used here is "noomah". This is the only time it is used in the Old Testament. It is a slumber or light sleep unlike any normal sleep pattern. A Psychologist would say that he is in an "altered state of consciousness". The average bystander would say he was in a "stupor", which happens to be a suspension of sensibility. He makes no sense and cannot make sense of anything. He is out of touch with reality and unable to be of any use to himself or others. The Scripture instructs us not to "mix" with this type of person, for it is imperative to guard our heart and keep it from risk.

The Prophet Hosea in the fourth chapter and eleventh verse pairs wine and har- lotry as enemies of the *heart*. "Harlotry, wine, and new wine, enslave the heart".

Any form of fornication, at any time, and for any reason will "enslave" the heart. Instead of the word "enslave", the King James and New American Standard versions use the term "take away". Perhaps you remember the Television mini-series which aired in 1977. It was based on *Roots*, a novel written in 1976 by Alex Hailey. Early in the show, Kunta Kente an African boy is being chased by Kado Touray, another African, with the intent to sell him into slavery. After a long pursuit the older overtakes the younger and is taken away to a slave ship headed for America. In the same way, our actions of infidelity and any sexual sin sell us into slavery and greatly damage the heart. No matter how long the chase, the heart will ultimately be brought into bondage.

The heart faces the same end if we indulge in "wine and new wine". This may seem harsh, but Daniel and other great men of God in Scripture were eager to avoid anything that might diminish their effectiveness for God's glory. The argument on whether consuming wine is proper for Christians has heated up in recent years. It is not the purpose of this book to get into side arguments that would distract us from the "heart". But in this Scripture, and other previously mentioned verses, the heart is a key player in the argument. Old wine has the highest percent of alcohol! No, new wine has the highest content of alcohol! These are comments often used in discussions concerning the proper boundaries for drinking wine. I have heard it both ways. According to Hosea, both bring harm to the heart. *The New American Standard Bible* says it this way. "Harlotry, wine, and new wine take away the *understanding*". This is accurate. When we behave in this manner, we soon come to the place where we just can't think straight. The heart has cognitive ability. The heart is able to think and reason and come to a conclusion or "understanding". "Harlotry, wine, and new wine" create confusion rather than straight thinking.

Many a new Christian, formerly a "wino", having just been freed from the enslavement of wine; has been confused and discouraged by observing a veteran Christian drinking wine. My personal desire, at any cost, is to protect my heart, as well as the hearts of others. Paul said it well in his first letter to the Corinthian church. The argument that Paul addressed was whether it was proper for believers to eat meat that had been offered to idols. Please read the eight chapter of this epistle, which is summed up in the thirteenth verse. "Therefore, if food makes my brother stumble, I will never again eat meat, lest I make my brother stumble". Every decision and action can be measured by Jesus Christ's summation of the commandments of God. "You shall love the Lord *your* God with *all your heart*, with all your soul, and with all your mind. This is the first and great commandment. And the second is like it: You shall *love* your neighbor as yourself. On these two commandments hang all the Law and the Prophets" (Matthew 22:37-40). Let's allow Jesus to have the last word.

COMMON DAILY ACTIVITIES THAT ENRICH THE HEART

There are many more passages in the Bible that illuminate very simple things in our daily activities that bring vitality to the heart. When these actions are taken our entire body and soul are energized. Let's take a look at a few of these passages.

> "And after Boaz had *eaten* and *drunk*, and his **heart** was cheerful, he went to lie down at the end of the heap of grain; and she came softly, uncovered his feet, and lay down." RUTH 3:7

> "And I (Abraham) will bring a morsel of bread, that you may *refresh* your **hearts**. After that you may pass by, inasmuch as you have come to your servant. They said, 'Do as you have said.'" GENESIS 18:5

> "Then it came to pass on the fourth day that they arose early in the morning, and he stood to depart; but the young woman's father said to his son-in-law, '*Refresh* your **heart** with a morsel of *bread*, and afterward go your way.'" JUDGES 19:5

These three passages share a central theme: a connection between food and the heart. The first passage is from the story of Ruth and her journey to Judah, the homeland of her mother-in-law, Naomi. Ruth is one of the four women named in the genealogy of Jesus (Matthew 1:5). She was from the heathen land of Moab, yet God chose her to be an ancestor of King David. The Book of Ruth is an inspiring love story demonstrating God's providential care. Ruth possessed many desirable qualities that drew the favor of Boaz, a kinsman of great wealth and prominence in Judah. My purpose now is not to retell this story. But I hope the little I did share encourages you to read the book of Ruth. We find tucked away in this wonderful story a very common and basic fact about the heart. The heart is made happy by eating food! I am sure it helps considerably if the food is exceptionally tasty. This Scripture does not say that Boaz was made cheerful, or his stomach, or his soul; but specifically, his heart was made cheerful. The statement: "the way to a man's heart is through his stomach" may be more pertinent than we ever thought possible. As an added caveat we are reminded that he then rested; which also benefits the heart.

The next Scripture in our trio of Bible passages comes from the life of Abraham.

Several significant conversations take place between the Lord and Abraham. In the eighteenth chapter of Genesis we find Abraham sitting in the door of his tent on a hot afternoon. He is approached by three men; two are angels, and one is the Lord.

Abraham is ninety-nine years old and Sarah, his wife, is ninety. Both are well past the ability to have children, yet the Lord tells them they will have a child the following year. The Lord also informs Abraham of His intent to destroy the city of Sodom because of their grave sin. Both of these two subjects of communication were highly important. Yet the first line of interchange between Abraham and his guests was just as important, perhaps even more significant. Abraham extended true hospitality to his guests. He bowed before the Lord, and offered to wash the feet of each of them. He humbled himself and demonstrated an attitude of servitude. He knew that the food he offered would "*refresh* their *hearts*". The King James Bible uses the word "comfort". The words "support" and "strengthen" would also provide a clear understanding on how the heart benefits from food. The point is that the simple experience of eating food can greatly benefit the whole heart. This is true of all elements of our heart. As pointed out earlier in this study, it is helpful in our thinking not to continually divide the heart up into different types. The physical, intellectual, emotional, and spiritual hearts work together as one, receiving and extending benefits as a whole.

When food is consumed in an atmosphere of friendship and hospitality, the heart benefits are multiplied. My observation today of hospitality in the local church is not favorable. I cannot speak of the Church worldwide, but have to limit my comments to my experience in the United States. Hospitality is on the decline. Hospitality is mentioned in Romans chapter twelve, where a list of differing gifts, given by God to his children is outlined. The Holy Spirit distributes gifts as He chooses, and every believer has at least one for the benefit of the entire body of Christ (I Corinthians 12). We should all exercise our gift whenever possible. For those with the gift of "hospitality" the example of Abraham is well worth emulating. He invited the three men into his home and fed them. This gift is greatly missed in the Church today. We all need encouragement to carry out the good fight of faith. To be more precise, our hearts need the comfort and strength gained from sharing food together in an atmosphere of hospitality. In his first epistle, the apostle Peter includes "hospitality" in his list of admonitions. "Be *hospitable* to one another without grumbling. As each one has received a gift, minister it to one another, as good stewards of the manifold grace of God" (I Peter 4:9, 10). I know that hospitality is not limited to eating a meal together. But when you "refresh" another with even a limited amount of food ("a morsel of bread"), you are comforting their heart. It can make a profound difference in someone's life.

The final Scripture that I am using to discuss the relationship of food and the heart is found in the story of a Levite, his wife, and his father-in-law. His wife left him and went to her father's house. She was there four months when her husband, the Levite, went to bring her back. The "heart" plays a significant role in this nineteenth chapter of Judges. It is mentioned six times. The first time is in verse three where the Levite "arose and went after her, to speak *kindly* to her" (NKJV). The New American Standard Bible says, "to speak *tenderly* to her", and the King James Bible uses the phrase, "to speak *friendly* to her". In the original Hebrew language the phrase is literally rendered, "to speak to her *heart*". The word "heart" is the same Hebrew word, "lehv" that is used hundreds of times in the Old Testament, and the focal point of our study. I can only conclude that the translators were emphasizing the need of the heart for tender loving care. Verses six, nine, and twenty two, address making the "heart merry"; verses five and eight focus on the need to "refresh your heart". This is in the context of the father-in-law urging the Levite to stay in his home a little longer before taking his wife home. Of course verse five is the main verse, emphasizing that a morsel of food will refresh the heart. The take-away is this, from that beginning point, this passage of Scripture continues to point out the need for a "refreshed" and ultimately "merry" heart. And simple things like eating food can bring about those results. Of course I am aware that there are other contributing factors like friendly conversation and a need for companionship. None-the-less, it often takes just a simple daily need like food and beverage to encourage our heart.

I think we need to be careful today in a world that continues to place more and more attention on what you should or should not eat. I am not saying we should stick our head in the sand, ignoring the facts about the harm from chemicals and genetic engineering that may be harming our foods, and creating a buildup of toxins in our body. I am well aware of the potential dangers. I am currently on a special medical diet that, among other things, is designed to remove toxins from the organs of my body. My health has been compromised for nearly a year. There has been tremendous improvement over this period of time and I give the credit to God, the Great Healer.

Things must be kept in proper order; God should have first place. The Apostle Paul in his first letter to Timothy encourages believers to keep things in proper perspective; putting their faith in God for life and vitality. "Now the Spirit expressly says that in latter times some will depart from the faith, giving heed to deceiving spirits and doctrines of demons, speaking lies in hypocrisy, having their own conscience seared with a hot iron, forbidding to marry, and commanding to abstain from foods which God created to be received with *thanksgiving* by those who believe and know the truth. For every creature of God is good, and nothing is to be refused if it is received with *thanksgiving*; for it is sanctified by the Word of God and prayer" (I Timothy 4:1-5). It is nearly a full time job keeping up on latest health issues of the day. In one decade a particular item of food is detrimental to our health and in the next it is beneficial. There is no need to be anxious; the believer holds the trump card. After exercising some common sense in food choices and preparation; say grace over your meal, declaring your thanksgiving to God, and trust the Lord to bless it for your health and enjoyment. A heart filled with thanksgiving is a healthy heart and a healthy heart is the number one defense against illness. An anxious heart is a stress filled-heart which makes the body vulnerable to sickness. Stay happy! "A merry heart does good like medicine, but a broken spirit dries the bones" (Proverbs 17:22).

Don't be Troubled—Sing

As I said before, there are many common, daily activities that renew and strengthen our hearts. They do not cost us any money and in many cases do not involve additional scheduling of our time. Singing is one of those activities. Not everyone has a great voice, but most everyone can sing.

> "And do not be drunk with wine, in which is dissipation, but be filled with the Spirit, speaking to one another in psalms, and hymns, and spiritual songs, *singing* and making melody in your **heart** to the Lord." EPHESIANS 5:19

There is a prerequisite for effectual singing. It is more advantageous to be filled with the "Spirit" than to be filled with "spirits". With this in mind we can be assured that our singing will not only benefit ourselves but other believers as well. True and powerful singing comes from the heart and ultimately is directed to the Lord. The body of Christ gathered together can produce a magnificent melody from their corporate heart to the throne of God. This is praise.

> "And let the peace of God rule in your **hearts** to which you were called in one body and be thankful. Let the *word* of Christ dwell in you richly in all wisdom, teaching and admonishing one and another in psalms, and hymns and spiritual songs, singing with grace in your **hearts** to the Lord." COLOSSIANS 3:15-16

Never underestimate the power of singing and the potential it has in calming the soul, and more precisely in calming the heart. I am reminded of the record of the imprisonment of Paul and Silas found in the sixteenth chapter of the Book of Acts. While doing the work of the Lord in the city of Philippi, Paul and Silas were stripped of their clothes, beaten with rods and thrown into prison by the local magistrates. The jailer put them in the inner prison and fastened their feet in stocks. That was some major suffering! We need to stop and put ourselves in their sandals. How would you hold up in the same type of painful and discouraging circumstances? Would you choose, as they did, to pray and sing hymns to God? That is the message found in our lead-in Scripture from Colossians the third chapter. What Paul and Silas needed was the "peace" of God taking charge in their hearts. And that is exactly what happened when they sang hymns to God, as the prisoners listened. A major characteristic of hymns is the generous amount of scriptural principles and doctrine that they contain. They are filled with the Word of God. Our heart is filled with the peace of God when from our heart, by His indwelling power, we sing to the Lord of his mighty works and love.

It enriches our heart and the heart of those who sing with us, as well as those who listen. To enjoy a heart "ruled" by the "peace of God" a healthy dose of singing "psalms, and hymns, and spiritual songs" is the prescription of the day. This medicine will heal the heart.

Since 1980 Science has renewed its interest in music and the benefits it has on healing. This is not a new idea for science but rather something modern medicine has let slip away. Some interesting facts were shared in the November 2009 edition of *The Harvard Heart Letter*. The article points out that music and healing have gone hand in hand for many centuries, and that the Chinese character for medicine includes the character for music. They share that music has a profound effect on the cardiovascular system by lowering and stabilizing blood pressure, heart rate, and blood flow through arteries. A specific example is sited in a study from Hong Kong, where volunteers listened to relaxing music for 25 minutes a day over a four week period. The results were lowered systolic pressure averaging 12 points and diastolic pressure by 5 points. God created music for the benefit of all mankind. It provides joy and healing for the entire heart, physical, emotional, intellectual, and spiritual.

> "Let not your **heart** be *troubled,* you believe in God, *believe* also in Me. In My Father's house are many mansions; if it were not so, I would have told you. I go to prepare a place for you. And if I go to prepare a place for you, I will come again and receive you to Myself; that where I am, there you may be also." JOHN 14:1-3

This is an excellent Scripture to conclude our discussion of practical things we can do to "keep" and "guard" our heart. Christ instructs his followers not to allow their "heart" to be "troubled". He is not saying that we should never be "troubled"; but that it does not need to be prolonged and allowed to fester, adversely affecting our peace. To be "troubled" means to be agitated, restless, and perplexed. When allowed to continue it becomes confusion, distress and fear. Christ Himself was "troubled" at the first level, but did not allow it to go deeper, and get a hold on him; "For God is not the author of confusion but of *peace*, as in all the churches of the saints" (I Corinthians 14:33). Satan creates confusion hoping to rob us of our peace. Christ was human and experienced the emotion of inner agitation and concern. In the Gospel of John chapters eleven thru thirteen we learn that Christ was "troubled" when Mary, the brother of Lazarus, wept over her brother's death. Christ was "troubled" knowing that He was going to the cross and that one of His disciples, Judas, would soon betray Him. But in it all, Jesus admonishes each of us "not to let our *heart be troubled*".

How do we "keep" our heart from "trouble". We do this by believing the promises of Jesus Christ our Lord and Savior. Perhaps the grandest promise of all is this one found in chapter fourteen. The path that we are to follow is the road of "peace" that Christ leads us down. I call this the road of "believing". To "believe" is to be confident, even persuaded of the truth, an unwavering conviction that your hope is not misplaced. In a nut shell, do you believe in God? If you do, then continue on by believing in Christ, His Son. Go on believing that the promises that Christ makes will come to pass. Believe His promise that His heavenly Father has a house full of mansions. This is not a lie, but truth in its fullest. Christ has gone on to prepare a mansion for each of His followers. Christ IS coming back! Christ is coming back for YOU! For all of eternity, where ever Christ is that is where you will be.

That puts a period on how to take trouble out of the heart and replace it with true peace—the peace of God. Focus your heart on God and His many promises. Demonstrate your gratefulness by being thankful and following His ways. Enjoy the wonders He has created in your life both now and in the future. Finish the race!

Ponder this in your Heart

To enjoy spiritual growth you must be resolute in guarding your heart. In what ways can you work with God to accomplish this task in your daily live?

CHAPTER ELEVEN | A Renewed Heart

I have used many different words throughout this study to highlight a heart that has been guarded and kept. It is a healthy heart, a whole heart, a clean heart, a pure heart, a peaceful heart, a strong heart, a courageous heart, a victorious heart, a renewed heart. All these are true and appropriately descriptive words. Eternal life springs out of a renewed heart—fresh and pure. The benefits of a whole heart are beyond measure, but I would like to mention a few.

ABILITY TO MAKE WISE DECISIONS

> "When wisdom enters your **heart** and knowledge is pleasant to your soul, discretion will preserve you, understanding will keep you, to deliver you from the way of evil, from the man who speaks perverse things, from those who leave the paths of uprightness to walk in the ways of darkness."
> PROVERBS 2:10-17

Making wise decisions does not mean you just get it right most of the time. It is far more than that. With wisdom in your heart you can consistently make correct choices. These wise decisions are often life changing and crucial to avoiding evil entrapments. The protection and care noted in these verses is initiated when wisdom enters the heart. The word "preserve" and "keep" are very similar. The word "keep" is exactly the same Hebrew word as "keep" in Proverbs 4:23, the pivotal verse in this study instructing the reader to diligently "keep" his heart. As mentioned earlier, it means to guard and watch over as a vinedresser cares for his vineyard or a shepherd over his flock. "Preserve" carries an additional perspective of fastening something down firmly with nails. If you "keep" your heart then your heart will "keep" you! It is a symbiotic relationship. It is a mutually beneficial relationship between you and your heart. If you guard your heart against perversion and evil, your heart will preserve you as well. Making the decision to be involved in any form of evil leads you down a path of darkness. The last thing you want to do is allow your heart to become dark. The right path is a path of light; for "…God is light and in Him is no darkness at all" (I John 1:5).

Complete Forgiveness

*"So my heavenly Father also will do to you if each of you, from his **heart** does not forgive his brother his trespasses."* Matthew 18:35

Peter asked Jesus a question concerning forgiveness. This verse is the final statement Jesus articulates in summing up the parable used to answer the question. Peter simply wants to know how many times he must forgive a person who repeatedly sins against him. Number seven sounds good to Peter but Jesus says "seventy times seven", which meant; never stop forgiving! Christ's meaning is clarified in the story of a wealthy man who extended mercy to his servant and forgave him of a debt in the millions. Later this same servant refused to forgive a fellow servant of a debt amounting to a couple dollars. Basically the ratio was a million to one. But literally even higher than that, as no debt comes close to the debt we owe God for His indescribable mercy. Thankfully we do not owe that debt, Christ wiped it out on the cross. The master was upset with his servant who was unwilling to forgive after being so graciously forgiven. He delivered him to the torturers until the debt was paid in full.

How could our punishment be so harsh, when it is so difficult to forgive someone who repeatedly distresses us? Or even worse, if they have hurt someone we love. I am convinced that the mind is not capable of fully forgiving, but the heart is up to the task. It is the heart that is discomforted in the first place, not the mind. The heart can fully and completely forgive. Christ commanded Peter to forgive "from his heart". The mind is often confused taking a calculated approach seemingly un-willing to forget the incident. But there is a big difference between forgetting and forgiving. When the heart forgives and the mind submits to this decision, the mind is then capable of remembering without remorse or any intention for revenge. Some things will never be forgotten, but they can be fully forgiven, after the heart takes the lead.

GENEROUS GIVING

> "Take from among you an offering to the Lord. Whoever is of a willing **heart**... All who are gifted artisans among you shall come and make all that the Lord has commanded...' Everyone came whose **heart**

> Was stirred, and everyone whose spirit was willing, and they brought the Lord's offering for the work of the tabernacle...They came both men and women, as many as had a willing **heart**... And all the women whose **hearts** stirred with wisdom spun yarn of goats hair. The children of Israel brought a freewill offering to the Lord, all the men and women whose **hearts** were willing..."
> Exodus 35: 5, 10, 21, 22, 26, 29

As Moses continues this record of the Lord's instruction for the construction of the tabernacle into the thirty sixth chapter, "heart" is used four more times, totally nine in all. The importance God places on the heart continues to amaze me. But it is not enough just to be in awe. The truth must change our life. Generosity must come from the heart. Generosity can be extended in a number of different ways. In the construction of the tabernacle a variety of things were given; gold, silver, and bronze were given. Thread, fine linen, animal skins and spun yarn were given. Special wood, stones, oil and spices were given. Jewelry and ornaments were given. These along with talent, skill, and hard labor were also given.

In his first letter to the church in Corinth, the apostle Paul uses the good example of the churches of Macedonia to motivate them to give liberally to the offering being gathered to relieve the need of poorer brethren. Again I suggest that you read the eighth and ninth chapters of this epistle. It is brimming over with valuable principles concerning the gift of generosity. What Paul teaches in these chapters could best be described as the "grace of giving". The first verse highlights the "grace of God" evident in the Macedonian Christians, being validated by their bountiful giving. Titus is urged to continue his work ("complete this grace")

A Renewed Heart

in gathering the offering, which required a great deal of travel. He is also mentioned for the care God has placed in his "heart". Paul encourages the believers as they have abounded in faith, in speech, in knowledge, and in love to also abound in the "grace" of giving. The motivation to heed Paul's instruction is found in the ninth verse of Chapter eight. "For you know the *grace* of our Lord Jesus Christ, that though He was rich, yet for your sakes He became poor, that you through His poverty might become rich". In the ninth chapter, verse five generosity is again noted; "...prepare your *generous* gift...that it may be ready as a matter of *generosity*..." In verse seven Paul encourages everyone to give "as he purposes in his *heart*, not grudgingly or of necessity; for God loves a *cheerful* giver." The mind tends to over-think this duty while a healthy heart is eager to engage in it with joyfulness. It requires the power of God to put charity into action. The King James Bible in I Corinthians the thirteenth chapter makes this truth abundantly clear.

Years ago my wife and I, along with our family of five children, attended a newly established church. At the end of a week of evening services, prior to the final offering, I felt led by the Lord to go down from the balcony, proceed to the stage and ask the pastor if I could make a few remarks. The pastor gave his permission and I began to exhort the congregation on giving generously, beyond what they might do normally. Then I proceeded to my seat and began to consider the amount I should give. I felt God was prompting me to give one thousand dollars. This was all we had in the bank. I turned to my wife and shared what I was thinking. She agreed and we wrote out the check and placed it in the offering plate. This was the grace of God working in our hearts. My mind would have spent hours if not days contemplating a variety of ramifications that this decision presented. The total offering that evening turned out to be the largest the church had ever received. We had a new family business at the time and God almost immediately blessed it beyond anything we had imagined. You just cannot out give God.

I do not have a special "gift of giving". God has graced me abundantly in other areas. I do have the grace in my heart to be generous. I just need to let my heart take the lead. "And God is able to make all *grace* abound toward you, that you, always having all sufficiency in all things, may have an *abundance* for every good work" (II Corinthians 9:8).

VICTORY OVER TEMPTATION

> "...because, although they knew God, they did not glorify Him as God nor were thankful, but became futile in their thoughts, and their foolish **hearts** were darkened. Therefore God also gave them up to uncleanness, in the *lusts* of their **hearts**..."
> ROMANS 1:21, 24

> "So I gave them up to their own **hearts'** *lust* and they walked in their own counsels." PSALMS 81:13 KJV

These and several other Scriptures associate the heart with lust. Yet our heart is the key tool for gaining victory over temptation. In chapter seven of his gospel, the Apostle Luke quotes Jesus' teaching about a "good" or "evil" heart. A person with an evil heart ignores God and becomes vain and useless in their thinking. Their empty and unproduc-

A Renewed Heart

tive mind rules over their "foolish" heart. "The *fool* has said in his *heart,* 'there is no God…'" (Psalms 14:1) But a "good" heart is healthy and whole, quick to honor God, and instant in demonstrating thankfulness. A pure heart will not allow corrupt thinking, thereby enabling us to overcome temptation. A healthy spiritual heart desires to initiate goodness and righteousness, the exact opposite of the wickedness born in temptation. The battle over the thoughts of the mind is won in the heart, as seen in Matthew 5:28. "But I say to you that whoever looks at a woman to lust for her has already committed adultery with her in his *heart.*" In this case, the lust of an illicit sexual relationship. I believe Jesus is saying that temptation will become sin when it settles in the heart. "Do not *lust* after her beauty in your *heart,* nor let her allure you with her eyelids" (Proverbs 6:25).

"Lust" is the desire for the gratification of carnal appetite. In itself the mind cannot win over temptation, mainly because the temptation is ultimately aimed at the heart. There is no doubt that our straying thoughts are first to pick up on the temptation. If the mind is properly yoked to the heart the temptation will go no further. Martin Luther was quoted as saying: "You cannot stop birds from flying over your head, but you can stop them from building a nest in your hair". These temptations flittering across our mind need not be allowed to take up residence. A strong heart will guard against that fate. There are a variety of lusts that tempt our soul; they are not all sexual in nature. Another of these inordinate desires is mentioned in Psalms 78:18. "And they tempted God in their *heart* by asking meat for their lust" (KJV). Three major categories are revealed in I John 2:16. "For all that is in the world—the *lust* of the flesh, the *lust* of the eyes, and the pride of life—is not of the Father but is of the world". The strength to deny the world and fully seek God and His Kingdom is found in the heart. "You shall love the Lord your God with all your *heart*, with all your soul, and with all your mind" (Matthew 22:37). If we do not give our hearts fully to God we risk the fate of being harnessed by worldly thinking, resulting in the entrapment of lust. "So I gave them up unto their own *hearts' lust* and they walked in their own counsels." Let your heart take the lead in fully loving God, and your mind will follow, as your soul experiences victory over the temptations of the world.

VICTORY OVER CONFUSION AND DOUBT

> "Of Zebulun, such as went forth to battle, expert in war, with all instruments of war, fifty thousand, which could *keep rank;* they were not of *double* **heart**. All these men of war, that could *keep rank*, came with a *perfect* **heart** to Hebron, to make David king over Israel and all the rest also of Israel were of one **heart** to make David king."
> I CHRONICLES 12:33, 38 KJV

A great deal of truth concerning the heart can be gleaned from these two verses. King Saul had just died and David's personal army of mighty warriors was rapidly growing. In this passage we see the hearts of men united in forming a monumental event in history. Momentum was escalating quickly in their quest to put David on the throne of Israel. Here were fifty thousand men who could "keep rank". They each possessed enough discipline that together they could march in battle formation. Individually they did not have a "double heart" but maintained an "undivided heart"

(NASV), allowing them to be of "one heart" in their pursuit of excellence. Each of these men had a "perfect" heart. That did not mean they were men who never transgressed against God. They were not men who completely avoided making wrong decisions. But they were certainly on the path of becoming highly mature in their thinking and conduct. In this text, the word "perfect" in the original Hebrew is "shahlehm". Shahlehm means complete and whole and stable. A "perfect" chord in music is a "completed" tone; it is a "whole" sound. The New American Standard Bible says these men were "stouthearted".

Years ago Dean Jones starred in the movie *Snowball Express*. The family dog in this movie was a large Saint Bernard named Stout Heart. The dog actually was not "stout hearted". He was exactly the opposite. He was warm, devoted, and affectionate; but also timid, cowardly, and fearful. A dog this large and fragile of heart is capable of creating considerable turmoil which is depicted throughout the story. We certainly do not want a heart that creates confusion, but rather a strong and mature heart that shapes order and confidence out of chaos.

> "If any of you lacks wisdom, let him ask of God… But let him ask in faith with no *doubting*, for he who *doubts*, is like a wave of the sea driven and tossed by the wind. For let not that man suppose that he will receive anything from the Lord; he is a *double-minded* man, unstable in all his ways."
> JAMES 1:5-8

> "Draw near to God and He will draw near to you, cleanse your hands, you sinners and purify your **hearts**, you *double-minded*." JAMES 4:8

This is a fantastic New Testament cross reference for the passage in I Chronicles. When I Chronicles uses the term "double heart" the apostle James uses the word "double-minded". Essentially it means the same thing. "Doubting" pulls us in differing directions. Instead of being secure and sure-footed in faith we are "tossed" about by doubt, unable to gain any wisdom or understanding for the challenges we face. Uncertainty and disorder does not originate with God. "For God is not the author of confusion but of peace…" (I Corinthians 14:33). So what is the answer? Seek God and change your behavior and your heart. God instructs us to exercise our will for positive change. There is something we can contribute after drawing our strength from the Lord. We must choose to turn our backs on any corrupt or debase activity, whether initiated by ourselves or others. In modern vernacular, we need to clean up our act. To be totally free from a mind that wavers, we are advised to "purify" our "hearts". Having a pure heart means that we have chosen to abstain from evil, immorality, and wickedness. The heart cannot tolerate one foot in the kingdom and one foot in the world. "Adulterers and adulteresses! Do you not know that friendship with the world is enmity with God? Whoever therefore wants to be a friend of the world makes himself an enemy of God" (James 4:4). Being a friend with God is a giant benefit, it purifies the heart, culminating in a single-minded intellect.

TRUE HUMILITY

"*Create* in me a *clean* heart, O God, and renew a steadfast spirit within me. The sacrifices of God

are a broken spirit, a broken and *contrite* **heart**—these, O God, You will not despise."
PSALMS 51:10, 17

"...I dwell in the high and holy place, with him who has a *contrite* and *humble* spirit, to revive the spirit of the humble, and to revive the **heart** of the *contrite* ones." ISAIAH 57:15

These two chapters are among my favorites in the Bible, and they have been for many years. I would encourage you to stop now and read them in their entirety before continuing on.

Much of King David's strength and success rested in his humility. He was quick to openly admit his failings before God and others and ask forgiveness. He was man enough to admit when he was wrong. He even recorded these experiences in the Book of Psalms for generations after him to read. Chapter fifty-one is the best example. This is the psalm of prayer that David composed after the prophet Nathan rebuked him for his sin of adultery with Bathsheba and the murder of her husband Uriah. He cries out for mercy and forgiveness from God. He is also clearly aware that through these sins he has damaged his heart. He asks God to "create" in him a new, clean heart. The word "create" used in this psalm is the same word used in Genesis, when God records the creation of the earth, the heavens and all that are in them. "Create" ("buhrah") means to produce something new. David is not asking God to repair his heart. He is asking God to create in him a brand new heart. That is a huge request, but it comes from a humble man of great faith. The "clean" heart that David desires is "broken" and "contrite". "Contrite" literally means to be crushed and broken into very small pieces even into dust. Pride is unable to abide in such a heart, only humility. This is the description of the "humble" heart found in the Book of Isaiah.

"Humble" and "contrite" go hand in hand. To be humbled is to be brought down, lowered or reduced in stature. It is visibly displayed when one bows down to an-other person. Humbling ourselves before God is the first step in experiencing His love and power in our life. God inhabits "him who has a contrite and humble spirit". As the prophet Isaiah points out, even if our heart is "contrite" it still may require God's touch. It is God's desire to "revive" the humble spirit and heart.

The original Hebrew word for "revive" is "ghahyah", meaning to breathe and live again. To revive a dying person requires getting fresh air into their lungs. When God revives us, He breathes His life into our souls. The first step in breathing fresh life back into a broken relationship is often the speaking of three simple phrases. I was wrong! I'm sorry! Will you forgive me? The human mind often struggles with this act of humility, but the heart is far more capable. The mind rationalizes at a high pace, finding numerous reasons why this will not lead to a solution. Something else needs to happen first. There will always be something in the way of reconciliation, but the biggest hindrance is confusion produced in the mind. The heart must take the lead, and it will when allowed. The heart desires to experience the truth that God has deposited in it. "Therefore humble yourselves under the mighty hand of God, that He may *exalt* you in due time" (I Peter 5:6). No, that famous line from a popular tune of the seventies; "love means you never have to say you're sorry" is not true. Yes, one of the benefits of a healthy heart is the ability to humble oneself and say, "I am sorry". When we bow down, God Himself lifts us up—in His perfect timing. We have dodged the deadly bullet of pride and experienced the grace of humility. "God resists the proud, but gives grace to the humble" (I Peter 5:5).

Everlasting Joy

> "These things I have spoken to you, that My *joy* may remain in you, and that your *joy* may be full." JOHN 15:11

> "Therefore you now have sorrow; but I will see you again and your **heart** will *rejoice* and your *joy* no one will take from you." JOHN 16:22

A heart that rejoices with the joy of the Lord, relentlessly generates a glorious life. The context of these verses is the occasion of Christ telling His disciples that they will face persecution. But even in suffering our joy can be uninterrupted. This is a special emotion, much more than embracing momentary happiness. It has as its source the Lord Jesus Christ Himself. This is Christ's Joy that He gives to all His disciples, to all His followers and is created by God that it may "remain". This is the central point of these verses. Christ's joy becomes our joy, a joy that remains with us constantly. The word "remains" can be likened to someone taking up residence in their dream home. They have no intention of ever leaving. The joy Christ imparts, fills our hearts completely, and begins when we accept Him into our hearts. And it continues today, lasting throughout eternity.

A Smarter Heart

Why then do so many Christians struggle to maintain a sense of happiness? Why can't we all be like Pollyanna and live in the "glad town", habitually looking on the bright side just as Pollyanna's missionary father did? We must deposit the promises of God deep in the midst of our heart. We don't just mull them around in our mind, if we truly desire to live in His blessing. In the story Pollyanna's father studied every "glad" verse in the Bible, and it blessed his life. He passed this blessing on to his daughter. Do not over-think it! By faith, accept God's promises in your heart. Do not be accused of being "too smart for your own good". Christ said that when He was seen after His return, His disciples would rejoice in their hearts. Rejoicing is the emotion of joy flowing from our heart. This joy in our heart is a reality because Christ did return from His crucifixion on the cross and burial in a tomb. He was resurrected from the dead. And even in His suffering on the cross, joy carried Him through. "…Jesus…for the *joy* that was set before Him endured the cross" (Hebrews 12:2). The same joy that He possessed has been given to each of us who believe in Him.

Jesus explains this truth in a parable illustrating the kingdom of heaven. On the occasion of leaving on an extended trip, the master left his servants in charge of his estate. When he returned he rewarded the servants who were faithful to him in his absence. "…well done, good and faithful servant…enter into the *joy* of the Lord" (Matthew 25:12).

The closing admonitions in the Epistle of Jude, verse twenty four, magnifies the hope of joy. "Now to Him who is able to keep you from stumbling, and to present you faultless before the presence of His glory with exceeding joy". We have the confidence of uninterrupted joy, now and for eternity, because God promises that no one will take it away (16:22). No one is capable of appropriating, removing, or destroying the joy of the Lord in our heart. God not only makes promises but He keeps all of them. Think of it! Your heart is capable of constant rejoicing. Your mind may not immediately accept this blessing, but you can quickly experience it in your heart.

We have not yet seen the return of Christ. While we fervently wait for His second coming the Holy Spirit abides in our hearts; supplying us with joy, hope, encouragement, and patient anticipation of His soon return. "…Though now you do not see Him, yet believing, you *rejoice* with *joy* inexpressible and full of glory" (I Peter 1:8). Words are simply inadequate when it comes to explaining the joy of the Lord. Even when coming from an over-flowing heart, words fail us: "…For out of the abundance of the *heart* the mouth speaks" (Matthew 12:34). The redeemed heart is powerful, but it cannot find the words to describe the joy it contains. Its joy is your joy, indescribable and "full of glory". This is joy that comes from the Lord, overflowing with God Himself.

PONDER THIS IN YOUR HEART

There are many advantages in maintaining a healthy (spiritual) heart. In what specific areas of your life would you like to benefit the most?

CHAPTER TWELVE | Coming Full Circle

A large amount of Scripture has been used in this teaching on the heart. Now there is a need not only to come to a conclusion, but also to review and consolidate some of the principles covered. Chronicling Solomon's reign as king and the changing condition of his heart should do nicely in meeting this goal. Like all of us, his story begins with the contribution others made in his life, before he became the king of Israel. Any person who thinks they have risen to success on their own is quite mistaken. I agree with the remark that a "self made man is a poorly made man". One of those who helped make Solomon was Samuel, a priest and prophet.

He did not directly influence Solomon, but he did make a major contribution in shaping the life of King David, Solomon's father. God declared in advance that He was going to pick a replacement for Eli the priest. "Then I will raise up for Myself a faithful priest who shall do according to what is in My *heart* and in My *mind*" (I Samuel 2:35). God was speaking of the young child Samuel who was already ministering before the Lord in the temple. This would have never happened if Hannah, Samuel's mother had not cried out to God from her grieving heart, pleading for a son. "Now Hannah spoke in her *heart*; only her lips moved, her voice was not heard" (I Samuel 1:13). Hannah promised God that if He gave her a son she would dedicate him to the Lord all the days of his life.

Coming Full Circle

Samuel matured in his ability to understand the heart and mind of God, and was quick to do what pleased Him. Samuel often singled out the "heart" when ministering to individuals or to the nation of Israel as a whole. "Then Samuel spoke to all the house of Israel saying, 'If you return to the Lord with all your *hearts*...and prepare your *hearts* for the Lord, and serve Him only; He will deliver you from the hand of the Philistines'" (I Samuel 7:3). God gave Samuel the ability to see into the future, which he used to direct the lives of those chosen of God. Before anointing Saul as Israel's first king Samuel revealed this gifting. "Samuel answered Saul and said, 'I am the *seer*...tomorrow I will let you go and will tell you all that is in your *heart*'" (I Samuel 9:19). He not only knew future events but also what was in the heart of Saul. He was not a mind reader, he was a heart reader. As the people of Israel continued to stray from the Lord, Samuel consistently appealed to their heart. "Then Samuel said to the people...'do not turn aside from following the Lord, but serve the Lord with all your *heart*...only fear the Lord, and serve Him in truth with all your *heart*'" (I Samuel 12:20, 24).

Samuel anointed Saul king over Israel and in the process God made him a new man by giving him a *"another heart"* (I Samuel 10:9). And although early on Saul associated himself with valiant men "whose *hearts* God had touched" (I Samuel 10:26), he strayed away from the Lord in disobedience. Later God commissioned Samuel to anoint someone to replace Saul whom the Lord had rejected. Relying too much on past experience, Samuel was looking for a handsome man of large stature like Saul. One by one he looked over Jesse's boys not finding a suitable one in the lot. They qualified in outward appearance but did not have the heart God required. "Do not look at his appearance or at his physical stature...for the Lord does not see as man sees; for man looks at the outward appearance, but the Lord looks at the *heart*" (I Samuel 16:7). The youngest son David was eventually chosen and would come to be known as "a man after My own *heart*" (Acts 13:22).

> "I know also, my God, that You test the **heart** and have pleasure in uprightness. As for me, in the uprightness of my **heart** I have willingly offered all these things; and now with joy I have seen Your people, who are present here to offer willingly to You. O Lord God of Abraham, Isaac, and Israel, our fathers, keep this forever in the intent of the thoughts of the **heart** of Your people, and fix their **heart** toward You. And give my son Solomon a *loyal* **heart** to keep Your commandments and Your testimonies and Your statutes, to do all these things, and to build the temple for which I have made provision." I CHRONICLES 29:17-19

A solid foundation for a loyal heart has been laid in David's life and his heart would soon have a direct impact on the heart of his son Solomon. David did not live a perfect life, in fact as is well known, he failed miserably. But he repented quickly keeping his heart in tack. The ending of David's reign as king reveals a man with a healthy, whole heart. His desire was to build a temple for the Lord but that endeavor was passed on to his son Solomon who would soon become king. In his closing remarks before leaving the throne King David refers to the "heart" nine times. He begins by revealing that it was in his "heart" to build the temple. Immediately after in I Chronicles 28:9 David gives his son some advice: "...know the God of your father, and serve Him with a *loyal heart* and with a willing mind; for the Lord searches all *hearts* and understands all the intent of the thoughts." David repeats the term "loyal heart" twice in chapter 29 where his prayer exalts God and intercession is made for Israel and his son Solomon. In all three verses where we find the word "loyal" the word "perfect" is used in at least two other translations. The desired heart that David suggests is one that is sound and whole, and completely devoted to the Lord. King David precedes his son in asking God to do a work in the heart of Solomon. David lays the groundwork for his son's subsequent prayer for wisdom.

> "At Gibeon the Lord appeared to Solomon in a dream by night; and God said, 'Ask! What shall I give you?' And Solomon said: 'You have shown great mercy to Your servant David, my father, because He walked before You in truth, in righteousness, and in *uprightness* of **heart** with You... I am a little child...therefore give to Your servant an *understanding* **heart** to judge Your people...' 'I have done according to your words; see, I have given you a wise and *understanding* **heart**...'"
> I KINGS 3:5, 6, 7, 9, 12

Solomon becomes king as a child. Many bible scholars say he was approximately twelve years of age. He would have to grow up quickly. His maturing got off to a rapid start at this juncture when he requested a wise heart from God. How could he be intelligent enough to make such a wise request? As I alluded to earlier; his father David taught him well. By his example, Solomon learned from his father that a wise heart was vital if he was going to lead God's people in a manner which was pleasing to the Lord. The beginning of King Solomon's reign quickly shifts into high gear. God gives him an abundance of riches and honor in addition to great wisdom. Solomon started the nation of Israel on a path of tremendous power and prosperity. They became the most respected nation of their day. "And God gave Solomon wisdom and exceedingly great understanding, and *largeness of heart* like the sand of the seashore" (I Kings 4:29). That is one big heart! What was the nature of information filling his heart? Did it just make him a better mediator when judging his people? Did it cause him to be more astute when negotiating with other nation? Yes, and considerably more!

The verses which conclude chapter four list many of the items that filled his enlarged heart. And let us not forget; this is "understanding" tucked away in his heart, not the mind. He spoke three thousand proverbs and over one thousand songs. He had a full grasp of the sciences of his day: botany, biology, physiology, zoology and many other facets of God's creation. I am sure he had a great grasp on mathematics of all kinds since his, "wisdom excelled the wisdom of all the men of the East and all the wisdom of Egypt" (v. 30). He was more than just intelligent—he was heart smart!

Solomon did build the temple which David had in his heart to construct. Early in Solomon's prayer of dedication for the temple and the blessing for the people of Israel he reflects on the heart of his father David. "Now it was in the *heart* of my father David to build a temple for the name of the Lord God of Israel. But the Lord said to my father David, 'Whereas it was in your *heart* to build a temple for My name, you did well that it was in your *heart*'" (I Kings

8:17-18). Solomon high-lights the "heart" eight additional times while blessing his people, many of which exhorted them to serve God with "all their heart". How did the people respond to Solomon's prayer of dedication and blessing? "They...went to their tents joyful and *glad of heart* for all the good that the Lord had done..." (v. 66). All of Israel, God's chosen people, had a wonderful, heart-felt celebration week.

After Solomon completed the temple the Lord appeared to him a second time. Again the Lord admonishes him to follow His ways in ruling Israel. "Now if you walk before Me as your father David walked, in *integrity of heart* and in *uprightness*...then I will establish the throne of your kingdom forever..." (I Kings 9:4-5) The focal point of Solomon's success continues to be his heart. This will be God's standard throughout his life. He simply needs to follow the example of his father David. You might think that "integrity" means honesty and good moral. In this context "uprightness" speaks of honesty and "integrity" defines the heart as healthy, whole, and full of goodness. This is a revived heart that has been the focus of this study; a heart that must be nourished and guarded. Will King Solomon care for and protect his heart throughout his entire reign?

The next big event in Solomon's life was the visit of the queen of Sheba to his kingdom. She had heard of his fame and intended to test him with difficult questions. She came to Jerusalem with a great company of camels, gold, and precious stone and "spoke with him about all that was in her *heart*" (I Kings 10:2).

She was overwhelmed with his ability to answer all her questions and breathless when viewing his incredible wealth. She credited God for his prosperity and lavished him with some of her own substance which in addition to

her gold and jewels included an abundance of spices that was never duplicated. Solomon's great wealth recorded in the tenth chapter is well worth reviewing. This listing of riches is concluded by a reminder of its source. "Now all the earth sought the presence of
Solomon to hear his wisdom, which God had put in his *heart*" (v. 24).

Even though God placed the wisdom into his heart, Solomon still had control of it. His renewed heart was his responsibility to "keep". "*Keep your heart* with all diligence, for out of it spring the issues of life" (Proverbs 4:23). These are the God inspired words of Solomon. Can he follow his own advice? I guess not, chapter eleven records his downfall. God made it abundantly clear that the Israelites were not to intermarry with other nations. "You shall not intermarry with them, nor they with you. Surely they will *turn away your hearts* after their gods" (v. 2). King Solomon ignored God and married one thousand women who "turned away his *heart*" (v. 3).

> "For it was so, when Solomon was old, that his wives *turned* his **heart** after other Gods; and his **heart** was not *loyal* to the Lord his God, as was the **heart** of his father David". I Kings 11:4

> "So the Lord became angry with Solomon, because his **heart** had *turned* from the Lord God of Israel, who had appeared to him twice."
> II Kings 11:9

The point of being in the race of life is to win it. To win the race you first must finish it. Solomon finished poorly and he paid a big price. God appeared to Solomon twice, equipping him to not only run the race, but to finish it in first place. But Solomon gave away to other gods the very gift that brought him world renowned prominence, *"largeness of heart* like the sand of the seashore" (I Kings 4:29). His act of turning his back on God cost him everything. "Because you have done this, and have not kept My covenant and My statutes, which I have commanded you, I will surely tear the kingdom away from you and give it to your servant'" (I Kings 11:11). Solomon turned his heart away from God, and God took His blessing away from Solomon.

This is not a sad place to end our study. It begs the question: If Solomon, the wisest man of his day, who had two miraculous visits from God, is unable to "keep" his heart, then what chance do I have? Yet, the Lord expects us to triumph in the race of life. "Do you not know that those who run in a race all run, but one receives the prize? Run in such a way that you may obtain (win) it" (I Corinthians 9:24). How can I finish the race with my heart intact? Quite frankly, we have an advantage over Solomon. You heard me right. One very big event has taken place since the day of Solomon. The son of God—Jesus Christ came to earth to save the world. And that He did, by dying on a cross for our sins and rising from the dead to bring us victory over death. A wonder beyond human comprehension took place, even beyond the understanding of angels. By His Holy Spirit, Christ now lives within every believer. This mystery has been hidden for ages but has been made known to each of us who has accepted Jesus Christ as his lord and savior. "To them God willed to make known what are the riches of the glory of this *mystery* among the Gentiles: which (who) is *Christ in you,* the hope of glory" (Colossians 1:27).

But let's be even more specific. Our confession of faith

was made in the heart and must be lived out in the heart. "If you confess with your mouth the Lord Jesus and *believe* in your *heart* that God raised Him from the dead, you will be saved" (Romans 10:9). How do we know this is true? How do we carry this hope with us on a moment by moment basis? The answer lies in the heart. "Now He who establishes us with you in Christ and has anointed us in God, who also has sealed us and given us the Spirit in our *hearts* as a *guarantee*" (II Corinthians 1:21-22). This "hope of glory" that resides in our hearts by the Holy Spirit constantly encourages us through God's powerful manifestation of love. "Now hope does not disappoint, because the *love of God* has been *poured out in our heart* by the Holy Spirit who was given to us" (Romans 5:5). The power to "keep" the heart lies in the heart itself. Because we are "… filled with the fullness of God" (Ephesians 3:18), we have the assurance of a sound and productive heart, a heart that we can trust to lead us in the race of life and bring us victoriously to the finish line. The closing verses of the book of Jude assures us that Christ is able to keep us from falling. Ephesians 3:20 magnifies this truth. "Now to Him who is able to do exceedingly abundantly above all that we ask or think, according to the power that works in us". Every word in this verse should be highlighted. It has been high-lighted by a multitude of believers who have gone on before us encouraging us to run the race with endurance (Hebrews 12). Your heroes in the faith lived powerful lives for Christ because of the power within. You also can be an influential witness for Christ by allowing the love of God to pour out of your heart.

This life of glory cannot be fully realized by the strength of the flesh, as it was initiated by the Spirit, it also must be energized by the Spirit. Paul made that clear to early believers. "Are you so foolish? Having begun in the Spirit, are you now being made perfect by the flesh" (Galatians 3:3)? The Spirit of God dwells in our heart not in our mind. The power of the intellect of the mind will never fulfill the mystery of God within our heart. The power of Christ in our heart will! In their introduction to the Book of Zechariah, the scholars of The Open Bible, NASV sum it up soundly when they say, "In the providence of God, the temple of the human heart became the abiding place of God's Spirit."

This study is never ending because it is based in the eternal Word of God. But it would be best for me to end right here and allow you, a student of the Word of God, to write the next chapter. If you so choose, may I suggested you begin by meditating on this closing passage of Scripture.

> "For it is God who commanded light to *shine* in darkness, who has *shone* in our **hearts** to give the light of the knowledge of the glory of God in the face of Jesus Christ. But we have this treasure in *earthen vessels,* that the excellence of the power may be of God and not of us."
> II CORINTHIANS 4:6-7

PONDER THIS IN YOUR HEART

God desires to work a miracle in your heart. Could meditating on these verses of Scripture be a step toward reaching that end?

AFTERWORD

What would you do if you discovered a hidden treasure? Would you cherish it passionately, spend it generously and guard it intensely? I trust you would. And that is exactly what our attitude should be toward the treasure of our heart. Nothing of eternal value is gained unless we take God's Word to heart. James 1:22 -24 instructs believers to "...be *doers* of the word, and not hearers only, deceiving yourselves. For if anyone is a hearer of the word and not a *doer*, he is like a man observing his natural face in a mirror; for he observes himself, goes away, and immediately forgets what kind of man he was." Hundreds of verses from the Bible concerning the heart have been shared in this study. Hundreds more remain to be acknowledged. God has made it crystal clear that our heart is the key instrument for success in all areas of life, most of all our relationship with Him and others. The use and condition of our heart is an essential factor in experiencing happiness and everlasting joy. There is tremendous confusion and disharmony in the world today and there won't be a meeting of minds until there is a meeting of hearts. Beginning with your own heart, great and unbelievable things can happen in your life and the life of those around you. When we engage a renewed heart our perspective of the world will be brightened and together with others of like heart things will change for the better. A heart surrendered to God can make all the difference in the world. Go make a difference!

CPSIA information can be obtained
at www.ICGtesting.com
Printed in the USA
FSOW03n2025150715
8761FS